Economy of a Primitive Tribal Village in Manipur

By the Same Author :

- Village Development in North East India : New Approaches
- Rural Development in India : Retrospect and Prospects
- Rural Development in North East India

Author

Komol Singha (b.1972) is Senior Lecturer in the Department of Economics, Royal University of Bhutan, Gaeddu College of Business Studies, Gedu, Bhutan. After obtaining graduation degree from Guwahati University, he obtained MA and PhD degree from the Department of Economics, Manipur University, Imphal. He specializes in Development Economics, and at present actively involved in development issues. He was teaching Economics at Don Bosco College in Manipur and St. Joseph's College in Nagaland for two and five years respectively. His contributions include, three books entitled: *'Village Development in North East India'* (ed. 2009); *'Rural Development in India'* (ed. 2010); and *'Rural Development in North East India'* (ed. 2010). He has also contributed number of research papers in the National and the International Journals (including South Asian Journal, Journal of Global Economy), Seminars, and Newspapers. His research interest includes the study of Human Resource Development, Social Capital and Social Sector, etc.

Economy of a Primitive Tribal Village in Manipur

Komol Singha

CONCEPT PUBLISHING COMPANY PVT. LTD.
NEW DELHI-110059

ISBN-13-978-81-8069-745-6

First Published 2011

Published and Printed by

Concept
Since 1974

Concept Publishing Company Pvt. Ltd.
Regd. Office :
A/15-16, Commercial Block, Mohan Garden
New Delhi-110059 (India)
Phones : 25351460, 25351794, *Fax* : 091-11-25357109
Email : publishing@conceptpub.com.
Website: www.conceptpub.com

Editorial Office :
H-13, Bali Nagar, New Delhi-110 015, India.

Cataloging in Publication Data--*Courtesy:* D.K. Agencies (P) Ltd. <docinfo@dkagencies.com>

Singha, Komol, 1972-
Economy of a primitive tribal village in Manipur / Komol Singha.
p. cm.
Revision of the author's thesis (Ph. D.)--Manipur University.
Includes bibliographical references (p.) and index.
ISBN 9788180697456

1. Maram (Indic people)--India--Maram Khullen--Economic conditions. 2. Maram Khullen (India).--Economic conditions. 3. Basic needs--Government policy--India--Maram Khullen. 4. Rural development--India--Maram Khullen. I. Title.

James P. Grant School of Public Health
BRAC University

FOREWORD

The Book " Economy of a Primitive Tribal Village in Manipur" makes welcome appearance, for there are very few research works on the actual economic life in socio-cultural network settings of the tribal people. Dr. Komol Singha rightly pointed the concept of tribal village in geo-social identity where the tribal people are inter-locked in their land ownership system, production in gender role set, cropping pattern, and market facilities in the age of globalization of a primitive tribal community in India.

The book consists of eight chapters. Chapter 1 discusses the basic concept of village in geo-social perspectives, chapter 2 explores the land ownership system, agriculture, gender role set in agriculture, chapter 3 deals with the forest, environment, and water stress, chapter 4 reveals health, education and population, chapter 5 identifies existing institutions in the age of globalization and how these institutions are related in the village economy formation, chapter 6 examines the consumption pattern and its comparison with the income, chapter 7 covers the basic infrastructures for economic as well as social development viz; social capital in terms of customs, beliefs, norms and value system, physical infrastructure, and human capital, and the chapter 8 wraps up with concluding remarks. In addition, the author has given recommendations in the core chapters of this book for policy implications.

This book is based on in-depth research conducted by

the researcher using the different methods and techniques of empirical research in order to collect authentic and reliable information. The academics, researchers, and the students of different disciplines like economics, anthropology, sociology, social work, and development studies will be benefited from this book. This book also highlights the contemporary situation in holistic perspective of tribal people living in the remote areas.

It is my expectation that this book will be able to contribute to the knowledge of administrators, planners and policy-makers to chalk out an appropriate, pragmatic, realistic and meaning policy for the over-all development of the disadvantaged tribal people and their well-being.

March 4, 2010

Profulla C. Sarker
Senior Policy Advisor for
National Food Security and
Nutrition Surveillance Project &
Adjunct Professor of Social Science,
BRAC University, Dhaka, Bangladesh

PREFACE

The tribal all-over the world generally lives in the hilly and inaccessible areas. All the communities, including the most developed one in the world at present, were tribal at one stage or another in their development trajectory. Their economic life, which has a system of mutual dependence, and the influence of social forces compel them to live as a unified force in a demarcated area. But, the pace of development of the communities is not equal and enthused by environment including government policies, in which the community is exposed. India's easternmost State Manipur's ninety per cent of the geographical area is covered by the hill. The development of the State lies on the development of the villages. And the majority of the people of the State's poor live in the hill villages. So, the development of village has become an important area of research among the academicians, policy-makers, bureaucrats, and political leaders, etc. in the recent past especially the hill villages in India.

The book is the modified version of my Ph.D. thesis "Economy of a Tribal Village: A Study of Maram Khullen, Senapati District, Manipur" awarded by Manipur University. In the nutshell, the book tries to explore economic structure of a hill village, a lone Primitive Tribal village in India's easternmost State of Manipur.

At the very outset, I would like to express my heartfelt gratitude to my teacher, Amar Yumnam, Professor, Department of Economics, Manipur University, Imphal. Without his able guidance and efforts, completion of my book would not have been possible. He has taken great pains and responsibility in completing my work right from the survey till the end.

My special thank goes to my ex-colleague Karaiba James, Lecturer, Department of Political Science, St. Joseph's College, Jakhama, Nagaland. He helped a lot at the time of field survey and more importantly in providing necessary information of the village which could not be covered in my field survey. Last but not the least; I would like to thank Mr. A. K. Mittal of Concept Publishing Company Pvt. Ltd., New Delhi for his effort to bring out this volume on time.

Dated: 10-12-2009 **Komol Singha**

CONTENTS

List of Table, Figures and Photographs

Tables

Figures

Photographs 81-96

1

Introduction

The tribal all-over the world generally live in the hilly and inaccessible areas. All the communities, including the most developed one in the world at present, were tribal at one stage or another in their development trajectory. Economic life, which has a system of mutual dependence, and the influence of social forces compel them to live as a unified force in a demarcated area. This process led to village life in the human history. Village communities all over the world have a number of common features. The village settlement being an independent unit, community life therein is characterised by the interaction among social, economic, political and cultural institutions. Notwithstanding the existence of class and groups inside the village, people of the village can, and often do, face the outside world as an organised, compact whole. However, they vary greatly in their internal structure and organization, in their ethos and world-view, in their life-ways and thought-ways, on account of a variety of factors. Among others, the factors of size - population, land area, ethnic composition, pattern of land ownership, the structure of authority and power-hierarchy, the degree of isolation from or contact with urban areas, and local traditions account for this diversity in their structures (Dube 1978). The physical character of a village is influenced by its dynamic interaction with the principle and pattern of settlement (Madan 2004:13). In the case of tribal communities, they live mainly on the hill tops due to various factors.[1] In Manipur the majority of the tribal population live in the villages particularly in the hills.

Topographically, the State of Manipur has an area of 22,327 sq. km., of which 20,089 sq. km. are of the hills and the remaining 2,238 sq. km in the valley. In other words, about nine-tenth of the total geographical area of the State is hilly. These hill areas are inhabited by 29 tribes. Five out of nine districts in the State — Chandel, Churachandpur, Tamenglong, Senapati and Ukhrul — are in the hills. As of 2001, the number of villages in Manipur is 2,391 of which 1,901 are in hills and 940 are in valley.[2]

Although, people in the hill broadly share a common socio-economic and cultural environment within a given region, no two villages are the same. As Yumnam (2002) observes, despite having variations among the institutions from village to village, they are generally grouped into two on the basis of commonality of features and groupings of the communities on the basis of origins. They are institutions of the Naga group of the communities and those of the Kuki group of communities.

Manipur became a full-fledged State of India on the 21st January, 1972 but the condition of village economy has not undergone much change. This relative lack of dynamism is particularly true in the context of the tribal villages in the uplands of Manipur. So, the understanding of the problems and study of hills/tribal villages becomes need of the hour.

The colonial period particularly from 1855 till 1940s witnessed the transformation of forest dwellers into tribes and the process of transformation of tribes into castes. Ethnographers earlier described all communities as tribes. And the distinction between tribe and caste did not fully emerge until 1901 population Census of India (Singh 2006 : 90).

Concept of a Village

In the opinion of Haq (1973), giving a precise definition of a village is not so easy. The village in America or in India or in Africa must have different connotations. It is because of their social, physical and economic structure. And even in the same State, there are so many differences among the villages. Some are big and others are small, some are poor and others are rich and some are hilly and others lie on the valley. So, there is no single yardstick to determine a village. According to the Oxford English Dictionary, village is a small settlement in a country area. Still, there are some common features to characterizing a village. They are as follows (Chaudhari and Chaudhari 2005; Standing Committee on Labour and Welfare 2002) :

1. Remoteness in character.
2. Settled together in a particular area.
3. Settled by the people of same origin or indigenous people.
4. Their main occupation is agriculture or related primary activities.
5. Low rate of literacy.
6. Prevalence of traditional culture, belief, orthodoxy and conservativeness.
7. Backwardness of infrastructure.
8. Mainly consisting of only one caste/community.
9. Commonality of some economic fundamentals.
10. Lack of communication and isolation from the urban centre.

There are few related features common among the villages all-over the world. As a proverb says, "One needs to test one grain in a pot of rice to know whether the rice in the pot has been properly boiled or not.[3]" Similarly, one needs to cast a close look in a village of a country to understand rural socio-economic conditions of that country.

Concept of a Tribe and Tribal

As Sikidar (1990) says, the word 'tribe' is a noun and 'tribal' is an adjective. It is erroneous to identify any individual say Mr. X as a tribal. He is a tribe, which he belongs to. Tribal is their abstract value they pursue since time immemorial. Tribe is a clan while tribal is a living system. Hence, our constitution's Article 342 has enlisted certain tribes in the schedule. Those people of specified clan so enlisted are known as scheduled tribe.

Misra (2005) observes that the very word 'Tribe' in Indian context is of a very recent origin and a colonial construct. The literature on tribe clearly indicates that there was no term equivalent to tribe in any of the Indian languages. The groups were known by their specific names in the group of their existence and there they had specific roles and status. A tribe officially notified as a scheduled tribe today lives in deserts, river belts, the islands, in relatively isolated habitats but mostly in forests. In Hindi, the term *'Adi-Vashi'* or *'Jana-Jati'* (*Adi-* Old or Original, *Vashi-* People, which means original people) appears in place of the English term 'tribe'. In Manipuri (*Meitei-lon*), it is termed as *'Hao'* from time immemorial (see e.g., McCulloch 1859). It connotes the people from hill and slightly backward in all respects.

According to 2001 population census, proportion of tribal population in the total population of the country was 8.2 per cent. The largest concentration of tribal population anywhere in the world except perhaps Africa is in India. It means that more than half (say around 60 per cent) of world's tribal population are citizens of India. The tribal groups in India can be broadly classified into three areal zones namely, North-eastern, Central and Southern. There are more than

500 tribal groups in India; out of these 75 are identified as Primitives (Chaudhari and Chaudhari 2005; Standing Committee on Labour and Welfare 2002), and one (Primitive tribe) is from Manipur.

Scheduled Tribe and its Determinants

The tribes variously or successively were described in the census and ethnographic literature as hill tribes, primitive tribes, forest tribes and backward tribes. It was under the Government of India Act, 1935 and the Constitution of India that the nomenclature of the scheduled tribes emerged. The Constitution of India, however, gives no definition of tribe. The notion of the scheduled tribe has two aspects : Firstly, it is administratively determined by the criteria of backwardness and remoteness and it is a political decision. Secondly, all tribes are not scheduled, the presumption being that there are still some communities similar to the tribes, which are outside the ambit of the schedule. This understanding gains support from the fact that the listing of communities notified as the tribe under Article 342 of the constitution is an ongoing process (Ramamani 1988).

Though, the all Primitive Tribal Groups (PTGs) of the country are tribes, all tribes are not as primitive. A committee was set up by the Central Government in 1965 to look into the question of the definition of the tribes. According to the committee, primitiveness and backwardness were the criteria applied in framing the 1950 and 1965 lists of the scheduled tribes. It opined that tribes whose members have by and large mixed with the general population were not eligible to be in the schedule of tribes (Singh, 2006 : 90).

Primitive Tribe and its Determinants

According to Chaudhari and Chaudhari (2005), in this age of globalization, there are still people living far away from the main current of development, in forests ill-served by modern communication facilities. There are no schools and hospitals. These people live naked in small huts, eating root crops, fruits, leaves and coarse grains. They have not heard of the computer, air-conditioner, cell phone, internet, refrigerator, etc. They communicate by producing different types of vocal sounds, beating the drums, brass plate and so on to announce the happenings of their routine life. Very few of them are acquainted with postal services and letter writings. These people are known as tribal or primitive tribe. Robert Redfield, an American Anthropologist, defined 'Primitivism' on the basis of small, self-sufficient, homogeneous and non-literate society.

According to Deogaonkar (2005), usually when a tribal group is classified as a Primitive group, the following characteristics are observed :

1. The habitat of Primitive Tribal Groups (PTGs) is in inaccessible forest or mountainous areas, valleys, etc.,
2. They live a scheduled life[4], i.e. a backward life,
3. They are either in a hunting or food gathering stage,
4. They practice primitive agriculture mostly described as shifting cultivation,
5. They speak their dialect and the oral folk-literature inherited through oral tradition is still alive, and
6. The community adheres strictly to their traditional customs, traditions and social norms and is thus strongly ethnocentric, etc.

According to Gupta (2005), the then Census Commissioner of India J.H. Hutton, was the first of all who conceived the word 'Primitive Tribe' in Indian setting in 1931. Later, W. V. Grigson joined him in the framing of the guidelines for the welfare of the tribes. According to them, for identification of Primitive Tribal Groups, States (identification of PTGs is a State subject) generally have to follow three norms.

Those are as follows :

1. Pre-agricultural level of technology,
2. Low level of literacy, and
3. A stagnant or diminishing population.

According to the Ministry of Home Affairs of the Government of India, the government has adopted the following criteria for the identification of Primitive Tribal Group.

Those are as follows :

1. Population growth rate is very low compared to the rest of the population. They therefore exist as small communities.
2. The level of technological development is still in pre-agricultural stage.
3. The level of literacy is extremely low and is lagging far behind the average tribal. There is practically little or no progress of literacy among such groups.

Any tribe qualifying at least one of such criteria were stated as Primitive Tribe and on the basis of these criteria, 52 communities have been identified as 'Primitive' till the end of Fifth Five-Year Plan, 72 in Sixth Five-Year Plan, 74 in Seventh Five-Year Plan. Now, it has been raised to 75 tribal communities in the last identification of PTGs in the country. The last PTG identified was the Maram tribe of Manipur in the year 1993-94. But no PTG has been identified based on figures of 2001 census (Chaudhari and Chaudhari 2005; Standing Committee on Labour and Welfare 2002).

Tribal Development Initiatives during the Plan Periods

Tribal development is concerned; in the post-Independence era, the philosophy of tribal development can be best summed up in the *Panchsheel*, five principles, enunciated by Nehru in 1958 in collaboration with Verrier Elwin, Anthropological Advisor to the Government (Dube 1998; Saran 1997).

Those are as follows :

1. People should develop along the lines of their own genius and should have nothing imposed upon them. We should try to encourage in every way of their own traditional arts and culture.
2. Tribal rights to land forests should be respected.
3. We should try to train and build up a team of their own people to do the work of administration and development. Some technical personnel from outside will no doubt be needed, especially in the beginning but we should avoid introducing too many outsiders into tribal territory.
4. We should not over-administer the tribal areas or overwhelm them with a multiplicity of schemes. We should work rather through and not in rivalry to, their own social and cultural institutions.
5. We should judge results not by statistics or by the amount of money spent but the quality of human character that is evolved.

In 1960, under the Chairmanship of U. N. Dhebar, the Scheduled areas and Scheduled Tribe Commission were set up, which uphold the first principle of "*Panchsheel*" (Saran 1997). It may be recalled that, the Tribal Sub-Plan (TSP) strategy was formulated on the eve of the Fifth Five-Year Plan (1974-79). As a part of the ground work, it was decided that special programmes for the extremely backward tribal groups known as primitive groups should be taken up on the basis of proper identification on the lines suggested by the Shilu Ao Team. Complete funding of the programme by the Government of India was envisaged (see, Singh 1998). With the emergence of Tribal Sub-Plan, major development programmes of tribal people in India were initiated from the Fifth Five-Year Plan (1974-79).

Coming to Manipur[5], the Fifth Five-Year Plan (1974-79), embodied a larger programme with the total outlay of Rs. 139.70 lakh for the welfare of the Scheduled Tribes in the State of which Rs. 137.94 lakh were actually spent on this purpose. In this plan, in the centre, a Directorate of Scheduled Tribes was set up in January 1976 and to give a better impact and to ensure proper allocation of the plan provisions, Tribal Sub-Plan (TSP) was adopted at the end of the plan.

The Sixth Five-Year Plan (1980-85), out of the total outlay of Rs. 246 crores, a total of Rs. 231.85 lakhs were allocated for the development schemes relating to Scheduled Tribes in Manipur. During this plan, the infrastructure development for the tribes has shown an improvement as compared to the previous plan. But a lot has to be done for the basic requirement of the overall development of the areas, i.e. road and communication development and the infrastructure, etc., this is the primary need for the socio-economic upliftment of the people, which is not yet achieved.

During the Seventh Five-Year Plan (1985-90), both the Central and State Governments have been taking care of proper implementation of the programmes by introducing tribal sub-plan with sub-heads under the main budget heads in respect to the given outlays. The total outlay of the State in this plan was Rs. 430 crores and relative allotted share for tribal development was Rs. 400 lakhs. In addition to the State fund, Rs. 1,251 lakhs of Central assistance was given for the development of tribal areas. In fact, maximum share of the assistance was given to the education, art and culture followed by agriculture, horticulture, and water supply.

The Eighth Five-Year Plan (1992-97), was to accelerate the socio-economic development of the trial people by taking into account the existing socio-economic conditions. During this plan period, the total State plan outlay was agreed to Rs. 979 crores, of this allocation the fund flow to Tribal Sub-Plan (TSP) was 42.25 per cent. In addition to the expenditure for the State Plan, there was also the Special Central Assistance to the TSP areas for the Eighth Five-Year Plan period. The agreed outlay for the said period was Rs. 227.50 crores but the actual expenditure spent for the same was Rs. 239.10 crores. It indicates that the expenditure exceeded the outlay by Rs. 11.60 crores.

The Ninth Five-Year Plan (1997-02), gave due regard to the general strategies adopted during the Eighth Plan period. The basic objective to the plan remains the acceleration of the socio-economic development for the tribal people taking into account the existing environment and socio-economic conditions prevalent in the area. The strategy adopted in this plan period is creation of amenities through infrastructure development schemes, poverty alleviation through family oriented income-generated schemes and improvement of tribal talent through the implementation of research oriented schemes/programmes. The State plan outlay of the plan was agreed to Rs. 2424.39 crores and against this allocation of funds for the TSP areas was Rs. 1022.75 crores, which is 42.15 per cent of the total State plan outlay. The outlay under the special Central assistance to TSP was made at Rs. 28.75 crores.

The Tenth Five-Year Plan (2002-07) became a turning point for the development of Tribal communities in India in general and North-East India in particular. Fortunately, the Government of India when P. R. Kyndiah[6] was Minister of Tribal Affairs had announced number of Tribal welfare programmes on the eve of 60th Independence Day of the country. Some of those are :

- Development of Forest Villages has taken up for the first time since Independence. Rs. 450 crores provided for basic infrastructure facilities in 2474 forest villages, including Maram Khullen of Manipur.
- Enactment of the Scheduled Tribes and other Traditional Forest Dwellers (Recognition of Forest Rights) Act, 2006 aims at to improve the lives of the tribal and other traditional forest dwellers living in forests by vesting the right to self-cultivation of forest land for livelihood, right of ownership, collection, use and disposal of minor forest produce, traditional and customary rights; Rules of carrying out the provisions of the Act are being framed and shall be notified shortly.
- National Tribal Policy is being finalised.
- New Scheme of top class education for Scheduled Tribe students' (ST students) to be introduced from 2007-08 to encourage meritorious ST students for pursuing studies at degree and post-degree level in any selected government or private institutes covering fields of Management, Medicine, Engineering, Law and Commercial courses. A total of 635 scholarships per year to be awarded to cover full tuition fee and other non-refundable dues in respect of government/government funded institutions, for private institution with a ceiling of Rs. 2 lakh per annum per student and Rs. 3.72 lakh per student for the private sector flying clubs for commercial pilot training.

Coming to the area of study, the Maram Primitive Tribe

Project was first set-up during the year 1981-82 with a token sanction amount of Rs. 1 lakh by the Government of India, under the Special Central Assistance to Tribal Sub-Plan. Since then, an amount of Rs. 132.41 lakhs was earmarked for the development of this tribal group till the year 1999-2000. Against this allocation, an amount of Rs. 124.94 lakhs was spent during the same period (Mohanty 2002). Despite all these initiatives, socio-economic development of tribal villages in the State remains more or less same till date.

Description of the Study Village

Maram Khullen is the original village of the Marams, the lone primitive tribe (Singh 1998; Sahu 2002)[7] in the State. The name of this village 'Maram Khullen' is of Manipuri (*Meitei-lon*) origin, which means biggest and original village of Maram tribe (*Maram* — name of a hill tribe in Manipur, *Khullen*— biggest and original village). Sahu (2002 : 128) found that this village is the oldest village of Marams, covers approximately an area of 6 sq. km. including the adjoining forest, waste land and vegetable fields.

The village is situated on the top of the Maram Khullen Hill mainly as a defensive strategy since inter-tribe clashes were orders of the day in the past. It is one of the biggest villages in the State and the biggest amongst the villages of Maram with 432 households and about 2400 population at the time of survey of this research work. It is about 94 km away towards north from the capital city, Imphal and 25 km from the district headquarter, Senapati. It lies approximately 5 km from the National Highway 39 (NH 39 or Imphal-Dimapur road) in the west. In the south and just below the foothill of Maram Khullen, a tar road runs from the Maram Centre, which is on the NH 39 to Willong, another Maram village. *New Magaimei*, a Maram village and *Mao Pungdong*, a Mao[8] village lies in the west and north respectively.

It is believed that, all the members of the Maram tribe

inhabiting in different villages/towns today were migrants or descendents from this mother village, Maram Khullen. Almost all the historical monuments, relics, traditions, cultures, and customs of the Maram tribe are still alive in Maram Khullen. They speak Maram dialect and topographically, its altitude is about 3000 m (approximately) above the mean sea level (msl). Maram Khullen receives an average annual rainfall of 1467.5 mm. The relative humidity varies from 36 per cent to 100 per cent and temperature from 0.5^{0}C to 36^{0}C. The nearest market place of this village is Maram centre, which is on the NH 39 in the east and 5 kms by road[9] from the village.

Table 1.1 : Number of households and population

No. of Households	*Total Population*	*Sex ratio/1000*	*Average Family Size*
432	2374	925	5.49

Source : Survey

Formation of a New Tribal Village

Unlike the system in the primitive stage described above, for the formation of a new village in the Maram community, two basic criteria are to be fulfilled. Those are as follows : (1) Traditional or customary norms; and (2) Legal procedures.

First, in accordance with the customary law of the Maram tribe, for the formation of a new village, there has to be, a village Chairman and a Committee for the new village. Along with the members of the new village should organise an inaugural function of the new village. Representatives of the neighbouring villages[10] are invited to participate in the inaugural ritual ceremony, followed by a grand meal. The ceremony is celebrated by killing a cow or a buffalo and graced over by the priest of the mother village (the village from where they are migrating). The boundary of the new village is demarcated by cow dung of the killed cow for the ceremony, followed by laying foundation stone of the new village.

Second, under the legal procedure, for formation of a new village, a document of No Objection Certificate (NOC) is to be obtained from the neighbouring villages, where new village is to be formed. A written approval document is to be obtained from the mother village. Then, an application for recognition of the village along with the NOCs has to be forwarded by the King/Chairman of the new village to the Deputy Commissioner through the Sub-Divisional Officer, Civil (SDO) of the concerned district.

Selection of the Study Area

The present study deals with the 'Economy of a Tribal Village', a village of Maram tribe in Manipur. The effort has been made to select a village, which has the characteristics of backwardness, poor and traditional in nature. In order to understand a village economy, it is necessary to understand the institutions, activities and day-to-day life of the villagers. This is particularly so in the case of a tribal and not so highly commercialised or advanced village.

With an objective to understand a tribal village economy and keeping the notions of the characteristics of a tribal village in mind, the Maram Khullen of Manipur is selected for the present study. It is one of the biggest tribal villages in Manipur with 432 households and a population of more than 2300. This village is large enough to represent a typical hill village economy and other institutional characteristics for the analysis being envisaged in the thesis.

Besides the reasons mentioned above, due to the closeness to the highway, there is the convenience of visiting the village for survey. Moreover, Maram Tribe is the lone primi-

Fig.1.1 : Rough Sketch of the Village (Not to be scaled)

tive tribe " in the State and it is believed that this village is the origin of Maram tribe. Most of the known traditional activities of the tribe are found in this village.

Objectives of the Study

The overwhelming majority of the population of our country's poor live in the villages. The development of the State lies on the development of the villages. And the majority of the people of the State's poor live in the hill villages. So, the basic objective of the present study is focused on the economic conditions of hill tribal villages in Manipur particularly the Maram Khullen.

More specifically, the objectives of the study are as follows :

1. The present study tries to identify the economic and social institutions, like agriculture, trade and business, market, village council, other social and economic institutions, which the village lives on. And, how do these institutions work and influence in framing economic system in the village.
2. Secondly, this study is the modest attempt to understand the main difficulties faced by the village in economic front and its possible solutions.
3. Finally, the present study tries to know the role of external institutions, like government intervention in the development activities in the village, Missionaries in education, and globalization forces, etc. in economic development in the village.

Methodology and Chapter Scheme

The present study concerns with the economy of a tribal village, Maram Khullen. For the analysis of the economic system of this village, 200 households were surveyed on the random basis. Primary data were collected through scheduled questionnaires on land, forest, agriculture, marketing system, service sector, consumption pattern, physical infrastructure, health and education and community and social activities, etc. This field survey was conducted in the month of September 2006 followed by constant personal interaction and interview with the village leaders including nominated King of the village. Apart from these primary data and personal observation, the present study adopts secondary data publishe1 in the books, journals and other related publications of the government.

Chapter 1 discusses the basic concept of village, tribe and

tribal, determinants of Primitive Tribe, village and study area etc. Chapter 2, the following chapter discusses mainly primary sector. It includes agriculture, land ownership system, the role of women in agriculture. It is followed by analysis of the data collected from the field and possible recommendations. Chapter 3 deals with the forest, environment and water stress in the village. It is followed by the analysis of the data collected from the field and possible recommendations. Chapter 4 studies health, education and population etc. and followed by the possible recommendations. Chapter 5 deals with the institutions like, Market and Globalization in the village economy formation. Chapter 6 studies the consumption pattern and its comparison with the village income. Chapter 7 covers some basic infrastructures for economic development like Social Capital, Physical Infrastructure, and Human Capital, etc. Finally, the Chapter 8 wraps up with the concluding remarks and bibliography.

NOTES & REFERENCES

1. The reasons for selecting hill-top as their habitat will be elaborated in the later part of this study.
2. Directorate of Economics and Statistics, Government of Manipur, Imphal 2004
3. As mentioned by Haq (1973).
4. The policy of giving special protection to tribes was continued also in the Government of India Act, 1935, which created the Excluded and Partially Excluded areas. Thus these areas were enlisted in the Fifth and Sixth Schedule.
5. For tribal development in Manipur during the plan period, see in detail in Singh, M. R. (2006) 'Tribal Development in 21st Century : An Experience from Manipur' Mittal Publications, New Delhi, pp. 36-39.
6. He is also a tribe from Meghalaya, a veteran Congress M. P.
7. As on 30th June 1993, as recommended by State government, Minister of Tribal Affairs, Government of India identified Maram tribe as lone Primitive Tribal Group in Manipur.

8. Mao is a name of a tribe of Manipur.
9. The village is 5 km from the Maram Centre by road otherwise it is hardly 2-3 km. Because, the road that reaches to village is very curve as shown in the Figure 1.1.
10. Leaders of the neighbouring villages of the new village are invited on the occasion of the new village inaugural ceremony to witness the demarcation of the new village boundary, to avoid future boundary disputes.
11. Ministry of Tribal Affairs, Government of India has identified that 'Maram tribe' of Manipur is one of the primitive tribes among 75 identified communities in India and it is the lone Primitive tribe of the State.

2

Agriculture

In this Chapter, agriculture and its problems and possibilities in the village will be dealt with. In the course of discussion, cultivation system, land ownership system, cropping pattern and area, women's role in the cultivation, method of production and implements, followed by analysis of the study and some possible suggestions will be given.

Closely connected with the development of agriculture, there are some issues like, marketing and credit problems in the villages. Lack of working capital is one of the major factors responsible for the inefficient working of the farm and the indebtedness of tribal cultivators. This discussion is preceded by a brief note on the chief characteristics of a subsistence economy, which is expected to serve as background for the understanding of the nature of the problem and lines on which the discussion could be developed further.

Shifting Cultivation

When we talk about agriculture in the tribal hill villages, shifting cultivation comes first in the list. Shifting cultivation is known as *farming* in West Africa. In France and Belgium it is known as *Sortage*. It goes by different names all over the world. Among the tribes of Orissa it is known as *Dabi* and *Konam*. *Penda*, *Jhum* and *Bewar* are the terms used by the tribes of Marias of Bastar, Assam and Madhya Pradesh respectively. In Andhra Pradesh it is called *Podu* (Ramamani 1988 : 100) and in Manipuri (*Meitei-Lon*), it is called *Pam-Lou* and in other North Eastern States, it is generally called as *Jhum*. For Maram, it is called *Malung-lu*.

Table 2.1 : Main Occupational Structure in Maram Khullen

Main Occupation	*Total population*	*Per cent*
Cultivation*	736	31
Salaried	141	6
Self-employed	64	2.7
Working in private firm	95	4
Student	976	41
Jobless (including under-age)	166	4.9

Source : Survey

* Out of 432 households in the village, 282 are engaged in agriculture (65 per cent household are engaged in agriculture in the village).

Shifting cultivation is regarded as the first step in transition from food gathering and hunting to food production stage in the human civilization. It is the age-old practice of the tribal people or any other primitive communities. This system involves cultivation of crops on steep slopes; land is cleared by cutting preferably virgin forest, leaving the cut materials for drying and finally burns it to make the land ready for dibbling of different crops before the onset of rain. Cultivation continues for two to three years in succession and leaves the land fallow for regeneration of forest vegetation and soil fertility to be restored. Gradually, due to the heavy population pressure on land, the *jhum* cycle[1] of 20-30 years has been reduced to 3-4 years in many parts of tribal areas.

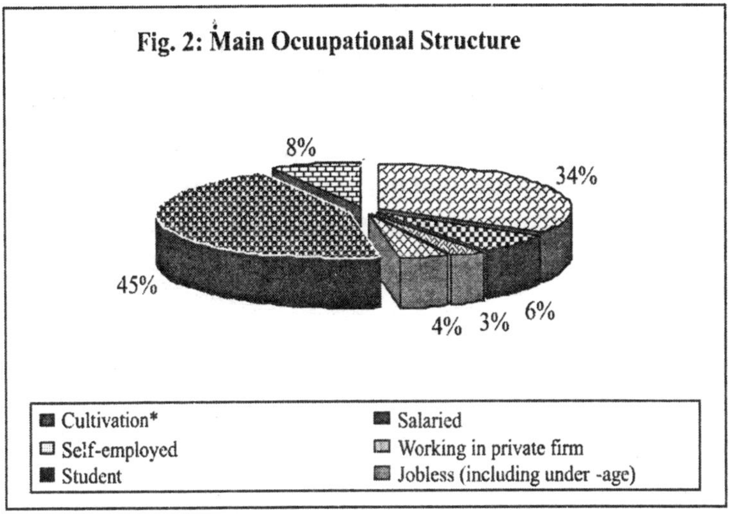

Fig. 2.1 : Main Occupational Structure

No longer are the Maram, particularly of Maram Khullen nomads, hunting for food and shifting cultivation have been discarded long before. They are settled agriculturists. Agriculture is the main occupation of this village and rice is the main crop in the field. At this present period shifting cultivation is practically being disowned in some other hill areas also particularly in Manipur. There are probably three factors for not practicing shifting cultivation in Maram Khullen and it is probably same to others too : First, there is no virgin forest fit for *Jhum* cultivation in the village. Secondly, *Jhum* cultivation is primitive method of cultivation and comparatively less productive. And finally, Maram Khullen has sufficient inherited land[2] for settled cultivation.

Land Ownership System

Maram Khullen is the oldest and original village of Maram tribe. Land use system of this village is more or less same with other tribal villages in the State. Land ownership system plays a significant role in an agro-based economy. Besides, types of land, policy and ownership system help in deciding cropping pattern in an economy. As the village basically lives on the primary sector, majority of the population adopt agriculture as primary occupation (Table 2.1), and even agriculture as a secondary occupational structure (apart from the primary occupation) of this village is pretty high, i.e. 3.07 per cent of the total population (refer Table 2.2). Nevertheless, there are some unique features in regard to land use system of this village.

Like any other villages in the country and in the State, the land ownership system of this village can be classified into four categories. Those are as follows : (1) Common village land, (2) Clan land, (3) Morung land[3], and (4) Individual land.

Table 2.2 : Secondary Occupational Structure in the Village

Secondary occupation of the family	*Total population*	*Per cent*
Cultivation	73	3.07
Weaving	385	16.21
Teacher	56	2.35
Business	9	.37
Others (including jobless, student and children)	1838	77.42

Source : Survey

The whole Maram Khullen is classified into three *Sageis* (colony). Those are : Mathak Sagei (Upper Colony), Makha Sagei (Lower colony) and Khullakpa Sagei (Chief's colony). Within the village, these *Sageis* (colonies) act independently in using their common land for the upliftment of the Sageis.

Each Sagei is again divided into two sections each i.e. A and B. Still, each section is further divided into different clans ranging from 4 to 6. Some of those are : Karang namei, Hoibi namei, Besii namei, Rairai namei, Bishung namei, Kannki namei, Pung namei, Ngiimei, Katai namei, Psiikatauba namei etc.

Table 2.3 : Size of Agricultural Land Holding

Size of land in terms of Alupak[4]	*No. of household*	*Per cent*
Landless family	13	3
1 only	90	21
2 only	188	43.5
3 only	111	25.6
4 only	30	7

Source : Survey

First, the common village land includes those areas which are too far for cultivation—forest land, cattle grazing land, places for worship, play ground, public entertainment place and land reserved for public purposes, etc. The village authority takes care of these lands and same are used for the welfare of the village. This common land/property is neither inheritable nor transferable, nor can it be sold to other village or tribe. There is one provision for acquiring village land that, if there is any dispute land of an individual with other tribe or village, which he cannot settle by himself, is normally handed it over to the village authority. The village authority fights for it which becomes village property.

Secondly, the clan land belongs to a particular clan and is passed on from one generation to the next. It has got a very specific significance as the clan always extends a helping hand to the needy and provides a portion of it if one of its members is in desperate need of it to survive. The clan also gives land to immigrants on the condition that the immigrant agrees to become one of them. The clan also generously helps divorced women or widows if they decide to live with them and remain faithful. This system of providing land to widow is no more in practice in Maram Khullen now due to the scarcity of clan land.

Thirdly, Morung land includes waste land, forest and woodlands, from where mainly firewood is collected for their common use. Sometimes, the land is utilized for cultivation of certain vegetables either for commercial or domestic use by the Morung members. It is not transferable to any of the member or to an outsider. Occasionally, fire-woods are also cut for commercial purposes for Morung fund. At times, the members of the Morung cultivate this land for common purposes. In certain Morung land, plantation of trees is also done as afforestation.

Finally, Individual land includes forest-land, *Jhum* land[5], and wet rice field, grazing ground and large grassland for hunting purposes. These kinds of land are well demarcated by stones, hill range, rivulets, etc. This is normally inherited as permanent property to the individual members. All these lands are held individually are inheritable and transferable. No restriction is made nor is any tax imposed on the community by the landowner for keeping animals on a particular land meant for grazing purposes. The forest and grasslands, which are too far to cultivate or are yet to be cultivated are reserved for future cultivation. These can also be utilized for hunting or trapping animals. The chest and leg of any animal killed in those forests by trapping are given to the landowner as tax. Nevertheless no tax is levied on animals killed with a spear or gun in the case of individual hunting.[6] No individual can sell land to other community, tribe or village; whether it is individual land or community land.

Table 2.4 : Rough Share of Land in the Village

Morung Land 8%	Clan Land 17 %
Village Land 25 %	Individual Land 50 %
Total = 100	

Source : Karaiba James (An educationist/Lecturer of Maram Khullen).

In regard to the succession of land, being a patriarchal society, the sons inherit land after the death of their father. If the father does not have any son, the inheritance right goes to his nearest male kinship. The eldest son gets some advantages although all the sons inherit the father's landed property almost equally. The house and the best-wet rice field will go to the eldest son and the rest are distributed among the other sons. Daughters are debarred from inheriting paternal land/landed property. Nevertheless, on the day of their wedding they are given a necklace depending upon the capacity of the parents. If mother has lands (given in her marriage by her parents), that will be distributed among the daughters. The only provision for a daughter to inherit the property from her parents is that acquired at the time of her marriage.

Individualization of Land

In the olden days, land was owned by the community in tribal society. There was no individual land as such in the past. The transition of community land to the hands of individual was, dates back to the history. There are many instances by other scholars in the past (e.g. Hayami and Godo 2006; Hayami and Kikuchi 1981; Hayami, *et al.* 1990) where large tracts of land in a village or over several villages have become private possessions through land accumulation by indigenous ruling elite or plunder by colonizers. The inhabitants of Maram Khullen are fortunate indeed to be blessed with forestland, agricultural land and pastoral as well.

The retrospection of the village history reveals that when the population was small and there had been surplus land for various usages, there was no controversy over land or no individual land as such. As population grew, land use by the people was intense; there grew a situation where the need of personal landownership developed. The tragedy of commons (as in case of environment) type situation appeared in the absence of a particular proprietor. This led to the selling of certain common land to private individuals to settle the dispute amongst the members of the community.

Another important factor responsible for transfer of common land to individual is, when a community wants to invest cash for common purposes or meets exigencies; the community sells out to individuals. This trend still continues today in Maram Khullen village.

Settled Cultivation

In the study of village agriculture, soil type, land ownership and variability of rainfall influence cropping pattern and agricultural practices. Three key features of agriculture in Maram Khullen are found. Those are : (1) the predominance of wet rice cultivation, (2) terrace cultivation of crops other than rice on the hill slope, and (3) the practice of intercropping.

This village from the time immemorial has been growing rice and it accounts for more than 80 per cent of the cropped area. Method of cultivation is concerned in case of rice cultivation; seedling is done at the onset of pre-monsoon rain, normally in the month of March. Seedling is done in a separate higher area, not in the cultivable land. The area for seedling is dug by spade after which the soil is burn with the help of firewood and dry leaves. It is waited for 2-3 days to let the fire be off and followed by sowing the seed. Transplantation starts in the month of June and followed by weeding from the month of July till August. Rice cultivation is done only in individual land. Harvesting season starts from the October and sometimes till November.

As regard to the method of cultivation, it is still crude that the whole area for cultivation is dug by spade only in the dry season before rain comes.[7] First round of ploughing takes place when monsoon starts with the help of buffalo. Second and final round of ploughing takes place after a week of the ploughing and followed by transplantation and weeding is done manually i.e. by hand. And at the time of harvesting, it is done with the help of sickle and cane/ bamboo is used as thresher. The threshing is also done in the field itself on account of the distance between the field and the village. After threshing the straws are left in the field itself because there is not much use of it in the village.

In the case of wet-land/rain-fed rice cultivation on the hill slope/terrace field, only spade is used and there is no chance of using livestock as these plots are prepared in small size step fashioned manner on the hill slopes in order to preserve water catchments (see photo 2.6). This feature does not permit the easy mobility of the plough. And other crops on the steep hill slopes are cultivated with the help of spade and dibbers only. One of the peculiar and interesting features in relation to river bed cultivation (see photo 2.5) of Maram Khullen is, during plantation and harvesting seasons, people have to go to the field and lodge in the small huts of the field, and returning back only after completion of the works. This is on account of the distance between the village and paddy field (River bed paddy field) which is approximately 10 to 14 km from the settlement (village).

Inter-cropping activities are done for the cultivation of Rabi crops like mustard, coriander, tomato, etc. These are sown in the month of September to October in the steep hill slope areas near the village. Marketed surplus if any is generated from this crop.

Cash Crops

Basically, Maram Khullen economy is a self-subsistence economy. They cultivate mainly for self-consumption and if there is any surplus, it is sold in the local market. Very recently they have started cash crop but still not in large scale. Main cash crops in the village are potato, ginger, passion fruit, turmeric, cabbage, and tapioca. Potato for market purposes is cultivated in a particular place called *Ragong*[8], which belongs to clan land. This place is about 3-4 km from the village on the north-west and it is very fertile and suitable for potato. Potato plantation starts in the month of February-March and harvest in the month of July-August. If it is for self-consumption, it is harvested in the month of September-October. It is because of the fact that potatoes harvest in the month of the July-August contains lot of water, which is profitable for the farmers. A potato farmer can earn approximately a total of Rs. 20,000 annually in average at the rate of Rs. 6 - 8 per kg (at the time of survey in 2006).

Ginger is also an important cash crop for Maram people. It is planted in the month of April and harvested in the month of January. Ginger stem and leaves are widely used in Manipur as vegetable. If it is for stem and leaves, it is harvested in the month of December. It is sold either in the local market or in Imphal. This cultivation is also not so large scale so that they can supply to the national markets outside the State.

Table 2.5 : Percentage distribution of area under different crops (Approx)

Food Crops		*Cash crops*	
Rice	70	Potato	30
Maize	10	Passion fruit	10
Other Vegetables	10	Ginger	10
Others	10	Others	50
Total	**100**	**Total**	**100**

Source : James Karaiba.

In this village, they do not practice double cropping particularly the rice cultivation. It is due to the two basic reasons. First, lack of irrigation, ignorance and physical infrastructures do not favour double cropping. Secondly and equally important factor is Marams have a belief that double

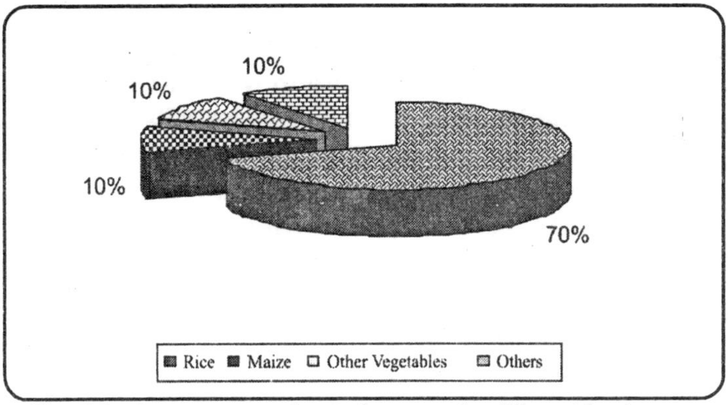

Fig. 2.2 : Approx. percentage of area under different food crops.

cropping gives a bad omen or bad luck to the village/society. This is the reason why they never practise double cropping since time immemorial. They do not still use fertilizer in the cultivation because they do not want double cropping.

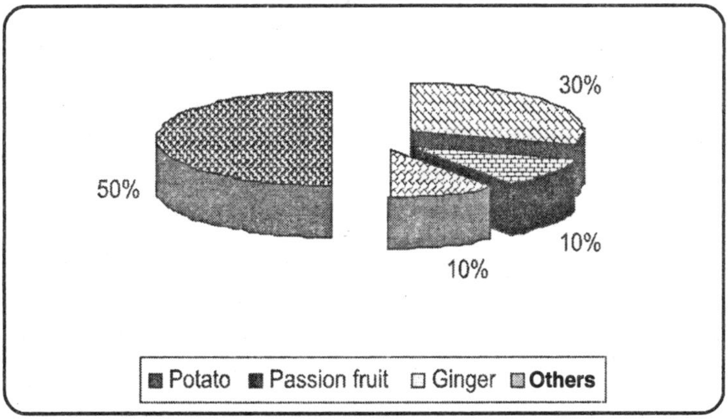

Fig. 2.3 : Approx. area under different cash crops.

Other Crops

Other Kharif crops like squash, cabbage, pumpkin, etc. are sown normally in the month from June to July and it goes up to August. Squash (*Biscoti* in Maram) is also very abundantly available in Maram Khullen. It is wildly growing without any maintenance. It grows on the roadside, in the barren land, in the bush, creeping everywhere in Maram Khullen. If it comes in the market price shoots up at least Rs. 3-5 per kg. Similarly, pumpkin is also growing wildly everywhere without much attention. Nobody cultivates it as a vegetable in a proper manner; still it is growing abundantly in the village. It is mainly prepared as a fodder for the pigs in the village and nobody sells it in the market.

Maize is also one of the most important crops in the hill villages and cultivation of maize does not need much maintenance and cost. Moreover, soil of this region is very suitable for the maize cultivation. In Maram Khullen, every household cultivates it for self-consumption and there is hardly any family without maize plant in the village. But no family cultivates it for the market purpose.

Similarly, cabbage is grown in this village abundantly and the soil of this village is suitable for the cultivation of cabbage. The type of cabbage available in this village and neighbouring villages/hill villages is very much different from the cabbage available in other parts of the valley areas of the State (see photo 2.3). Unlike round/ball type cabbage, it is like tree type plant in human height. Its' leaves expand widely like any other tree leaves. It is grown throughout the year and one leaf is enough for curry in a small family of 2-3 members. They cultivate it mainly for self-consumption and it is not considered as cash crop in the village.

Another peculiar crop in the village is Tree Tomato[9] (*Cyphomandra betacea sendt.*), it is a lesser-known vegetable grown in hill villages of Manipur and its adjoining areas. It is very popular and commonly used by the Marams, locally known as *Athingti*. This fruit/vegetable is used as a substitute product of tomato in various curry items and also for making chutney. It is grown abundantly in Maram Khullen without much care. It bears fruit when it is about 1½ to 2 years of old and continues to be productive for 7-8 years. The average yield of a tree is 10–15 kg of fruit annually and it is harvested throughout the year.

Horticulture

Passion fruit is one of such product, which farmer needs to cultivate as it has immense potential for export value. Though passion fruit is native to Brazil, it is found growing wildly in many parts of North East India (NEI) particularly in the hill areas of Manipur, Nagaland and Mizoram. Fresh ripe fruit can be eaten or the juice after extraction can be used for the preparation of squash. Its tender leaves can also be used as vegetable by the Marams. In Maram Khullen, passion fruit is cultivated in the mid hills to high hills. It thrives best under cool and humid climate free from extreme cold and heat. Passion fruit is very suitable in the soils having high organic matter content and well-grained soil. It does best in the sandy loam to clayey loam soil, which the Maram Khullen has. It is very productive fruit, total yield ranging from 10-12 tonnes per hectares annually in the village.[10] Harvesting period starts from the month of May till December. Two main periods of harvesting are observed in Maram Khullen area from March-May and August-December. It is being sold in the local market as fresh fruit or sent to the Exotic Juice Ltd. at Mao gate (Manipur) where the processing for passion fruit is done and then send to Bangalore for packaging, the drink brand *'Pasip'*.

Main cultivation of this fruit in the village is taken up in large scale by the Non-Governmental Organization (NGO) named International Fund for Agricultural Development (IFAD), its headquarter is in Rome. Maram has got a lot of clan land and village land, which are not properly utilized. IFAD gives loans to the co-operative farmers for cultivation of passion fruit and after harvesting the fruit is again taken back by the former for the processing at Exotic Juice Ltd. If any individual farmer wants to do the same, it is also very much welcomed.

Crop Area for Cultivation

Weeding, hoeing and the application of pesticides are not being used for rice cultivation of this village. But the productivity is quite high and the output is more than self consumption in the village. What type of crop cultivates in what type of land in the village? Crop area of this village can be divided broadly into four categories. Those are as follows :

1. Fertile and sedimentary soil type of land is on the river/river bank of the Barak River. It is about 10- 12 km from the village and it is the farthest land for cultivation of the village. This land serves as 'rice bowl' to the Maram Khullen. It is exclusively for the wet rice cultivation and almost all the people of this village live on this land.
2. Second type of land is the terrace cultivation area on the hill slope but not too steep. This land is also exclusively used for the wet rice cultivation. This land is prepared in a step-like manner so as to preserve run-off water from the upper hill slope.
3. The sandy and bit rocky lands are on the very steep hill slope. It is the nearest agricultural land of the village. It is basically used for intercropping purposes. This land is not possible for rice cultivation because of its steepness and run-off water/rain water cannot be blocked. Vegetables like potato, tomato, cabbage, beans, chilli, maize, cucumber, coriander and squash (*Biscoti* in local language) are mainly cultivated in this land.
4. The fourth type of land is very fertile on hill plateau used mainly for cash crops like potato, beans, ginger and for other inter-cropping purposes, etc.

Table 2.6 : External Assistance on Cultivation

Organization	*Year*	*Crops*	*Area covered*	*Price of Crop (Rs)*
IFAD	2001	Passion fruit	7 acre	8-10 per kg
IFAD	2001	Tree Tomato	6 acre	20 per kg

Source : Kuba Luke, Community Co-ordinator, IFAD, Maram Khullen.

Implements used in the Cultivation

The implements used in cultivation are mechanically very simple. It is mainly made of raw materials collected from the forest at zero cost. Almost all the peasants use traditional tools like Wooden Plough, Sickle, Hoe, Thresher, Spade, Dao, Yoke, Dibber and Leveller, etc. Almost all the implements except Spade, Sickle and Dao are locally available. The iron or iron-tipped instruments are purchased from the market.

The central and most important implement in agriculture of the hill tribal villages particularly of Maram Khullen is "Spade." It is used whether in the wet-rice cultivation or dry-land farming or even in the hill slope cultivation. The spade is found and used in different sizes and used for an endless variety of purposes. The big size is used for digging dry paddy field before monsoon reaches, whereas the small one is mainly used for dibbling seeds or planting Rabi crops/ vegetables on the hill slopes.

The wooden plough (*Abui-pote* in Maram) with iron-tipped at the edge is generally used for wet rice cultivation. Buffalo plays a significant role for the wet rice cultivation in the river-bed fields of the village, whereas only spade is used in the terrace cultivation. It is more labour intensive; own arm is used as lever. Human labour, particularly for tilling the field can be hired but the other forms of workforce can be borrowed from the other households. People who sell their labour power if any will not bring any implements. They bring only Dao/Spade sometimes if necessary.

Basket (*Arak* in Maram), slung over the back through a strip from the head (see photo 2.8) is a common instrument for transporting agricultural produces or other commodities not only in Maram Khullen but also in other tribal villages in the NE region. It is made of cane or bamboo collected from the forest. And for collecting paddy from the field after harvesting, jute sack is generally used. In recent years and since the paddy fields are quite far from the village, Shaktiman (Truck) has been introduced for transporting paddy from the field and store in the granary at home. The granaries are made of bamboo (see photo 2.8, right portion). Small huts (*Kaha* in Maram) are made in the paddy fields for taking shelter and even stay few days during the peak harvesting/plantation season.

Maize and other vegetables are harvested by hand but the rice is harvested by cutting the stalk with a sickle and after harvesting the straw is left in the field. For husking grains, winnower dish-shaped mat made of bamboo is used. And for poundering grains, large wooden pounder made of the knee high, wooden mortar and three feet long wooden pestle is used.

Women's Role in Agriculture

Though the Maram is a patriarchal society, the role of women is very significant not only in cultivation but also in other activities in the society. Unlike in some other States of the country, women have equal rights/roles in the society. There is no discrimination or any sort of exploitation to the women in Maram and all the NE tribal communities in general. Even if the men-folks in the family own almost all the lands in the village, women play equal role in cultivation. There are a few agricultural operations performed mainly by women; for instance, transplantation of paddy, seedlings and weeding the fields. Similarly, due to their inherent biological differences women cannot do some physical activities like, ploughing and driving Shaktiman (Truck). Still, the contribution of women is very significant in the tribal economy particularly in Maram Khullen. There is no area of work in cultivation where women's participation is insignificant. Apart from which ninety per cent of the women in the village do weaving at home as secondary occupation at their leisure times. They also do gardening and other domestic works.

Analysis of the Data

Agriculture still remains the most important sector in Maram Khullen economy despite it is highly neglected by the people of the village. Their economy is intertwined around agriculture and its related activities. We can achieve economic growth in the village only through accelerated agricultural progress (see, Swaminathan 2007). Agriculture practices followed by almost all the families in Maram Khullen are not managed on commercial lines. Rather, it is still maintained at the subsistence level so as to meet the requirements of food for the entire family throughout the year. Most of the working units are still maintained at the household level or household inputs. This trend has resulted in a poor show in agricultural practices. They have not started using even fertilizer so far in cultivation. This village has sufficient agricultural produces to feed the population. The average land holding in the village is 0.4 *Alupak.* Thirteen families in the village i.e. 3 per cent are landless and thirty of them (i.e. 7 per cent) are having 4 *Alupak* each. Average annual income of the head of the family in the village is Rs. 42,970 (approx.) at the time of survey, which is quite high in an agrarian economy. The average family size in the village is 6 only. Basically, this village is an agrarian subsistence economy. Backward sloping supply curve (Boeke 1953) of cultivation prevails in the economy. If one *Alupak* or two gives enough crops for a family to feed sufficiently in a year, there is a tendency of containment not to cultivate more. They cultivate according to the availability of the labour force in the family not according to the requirement of the crop. This makes indifferent for the 3 per cent of landless families in the village. They can till the unused arable land available in the village with any rent. Cash crop is not so much popular in the village because people here are not commercially oriented, also not forgetting that they consider agriculture as low grade in their profession. Weyland (1993) also highlighted the same idea in his master piece 'Agrarian Village in Egypt' in which many educated young people has taken up government jobs, which secure them a minimum monetary income. Though 99.07 per cent of the household are engaged directly or indirectly in agriculture, only 31 per cent of the population in the village is considered as main occupation.

As far as agricultural implements are concerned; this village uses almost all the traditional implements available in their village. Only the technology embedded in the agriculture is Shaktiman (Truck) for transportation of paddy from the fields and four mini rice mills. In 2006, a villager purchased a tractor for tilling fields, which has brought a bit sigh of relief to the cultivators and to the womenfolk in particular. They have not started using fertilizer. The idea of double cropping and irrigation facility in cultivation is not yet cropped up in the village. But the output is more than enough for self-consumption and still so many semi-forest lands are left unused.

To distinguish this stable, conservative tradition from the more recently emergent, foreign-influenced ways of the city is not to say that the rural tradition is fixed and unchanging. New ways are entering the rural community, some from the city or from the abroad via the city, some spontaneously from changing circumstances in the countryside itself.[11] Maram

Khullen is also changing rapidly in the tune of modern lifestyle. Need and preference of the villager are diversifying; subsistence economy type needs to be changed over time.

Maram Khullen has strong village level organizational set up. Village law is more firm and effective than the State law. Taking this effective village level or community level organizational set up and the availability of excess common land into the consideration, IFAD had entered in the village with a mission to start cash crop cultivation in the year 2004 in the village. Before the arrival of IFAD, not a single family could avail loan or any sort of credit, subsidy for cultivation. Here a question that comes in front of us is, despite having all sorts of facilities and opportunities, why does this village still remain in a primitive stage?

There is no evidence that a country can accelerate its rate of economic growth from non-agricultural activity when it is overshadowed by a large agricultural sector, which is pre-occupied with self-subsistence production (Haswell 1967:1). Agriculture continues to be the mainstay of the tribal hill villages of the North-East India. However, despite the obvious favourable agro-climatic conditions, various factors, some of which are unique to the region have been responsible for the arrested development and lack of agricultural growth of a sustained and widespread kind. Over and above the usual marketing and credit problems and lack of working capital, there is very little diversification in occupations and very few inputs are made to increase the productivity of land. The economy is of a subsistence kind and cultivation in these tribal villages is mainly for self-consumption.

The development of an agrarian economy is possible only when diversification of crops and technology is adopted according to time and situation. Different models have been adopted for the purpose in other parts of the world, e.g. *Farm-to-Market*[12] links are created. The *'Buraku'* community in a pine-covered hill village *'Niiike'* in Japan (Beardsley *et al.* 1959:3) is founded on the requirements of intensive agricultural technology and agrarian economy, which were dominant through centuries of Japanese history, and the same is found in *Horizontal and Vertical Expansion* (Radwan and Lee 1986 : 2) of agriculture. According to the recent district-wise data compiled by *Indicus Analytics*, farm output in Nagaland's eight districts out of eleven has grown at double-digit rates over 2000-05 whereas all India average is only 2.6. This is primarily due to a shift in cropping patterns (*Yojana*, Dec. 2007). For example, in the study of Gudeman (1978), total transformation of the people's economy was seen in Latin America due to the introduction of sugarcane by leaving aside rice and maize cultivation.

The study reveals that the Maram Khullen village is in a transitional stage from complete subsistence to cash cropping and influences to the transformation of people's life. Gudeman (1978) also depicted how a Panamanian village leaves aside planting rice and maize in order to accommodate cash crop, sugarcane. Though this sector has so many potentials and possibilities to develop in the village, it has three major drawbacks.

First, the importance of the agriculture has been declining, and diversification into services and manufacturing has been inadequate. As a result of which, the village continues to miss out the economic growth/ development at large. Even if 99 per cent of families in the village are engaged directly or indirectly in agriculture, they cannot consider this sector as core sector in their economy. Nobody considers cultivation as a noble profession; it is opted only when all attempts in life get failed. It is because of the fact that agriculture in the village does not give full security in the people's life. Technology or the very much talk about at present, green revolution has not yet reached this village.

Secondly, the quantity of the cash crop available in the village is not too big enough for export outside the village regularly. It is because of the crude method of the cultivation.

The crops become very cheap during the harvesting season and very costly during the off-season. It is due to poor agricultural infrastructures like godown/storage, marketing facilities, irrigation and fertilizers, etc. In the harvesting season, every family harvests the same crops so there is not much demand of the crops in the local market and quantity of the produce is also not so big enough to export to other city or market. They ought to sell through the greedy traders at the lower price. For instance, squash price in the Maram bazar or centre is Rs. 3-5 per kg during the season, which is same or lesser in Imphal city at the same period.

Thirdly, lack of work culture and seriousness is also a major defect in the agricultural activities in the village. IFAD had started community cultivation since 2004 with 13 acres cash crop in the village. It is not a small area in cash crop cultivation. But the result of it is in dismal and not appreciable. In the beginning of the project i.e. 2004, the output of Passion fruit was quite big even if the officials of the project couldn't give exact quantity. Even after the 6 years of the project, they cannot ascertain the production per acre in the ongoing project in the village. It looks little unaccountable of the project. At present, the work of the project in reality is not so visible due to the negligence of the people. Moreover, villagers are also not fully aware of the cash crops.

Though Maram Khullen believes in village/community law, it misses out the idea of economic development. For example, a rice-growing village *Niiike* in Japan could develop because of the well-organized village institutions. In economic front, village institutions of Maram Khullen work inefficiently. Institutions continue to function in a top-down manner and public sector goals are defined in terms of readily observed physical outputs rather than desired functional outcomes; "embankment length constructed" rather than "flood protection provided" and "number of schools built" rather than "improvements in learning quality" (World Bank

2006). The government or any other external assistance for the development of the village like IFAD project cannot function properly due to their negligence or ignorance nature of the people. Loans are generally treated as grant and cannot be used for productive activities.

More importantly, the pace of development in agricultural sector in the village is not up to the expected level. Despite agriculture being a source of livelihood, the people of the village cannot consider this sector as an important profession. It is probably due to the lack of innovation and unavailability of market of the products of this sector. Diversification of crops, hybridisation, modernisation, technological development and commercialisation of agriculture etc. are missing in the village. In nutshell, this sector needs institutional or structural changes in the village.

Some Possible Suggestions

The contours of Indian agriculture started showing improvement gradually after the mid-sixties with the introduction of High Yielding Varieties of seeds. The subsequent emphasis was laid on the development of agricultural infrastructures for supply of agro-inputs like irrigation, power, water, seeds and fertilizers, creation of storage and marketing facilities and provision of adequate and fair distribution of foodgrains (see, Tripathy and Jain 2007). The poor growth of the Indian agricultural sector was due to the deficiency of capital and the National Agricultural Policy, 2000, highlighted proper infrastructures. Agriculture being an important sector in the village, well-defined strategies is to be taken so as to make this sector more flourishing in the coming future. For this, government should take major initiatives to develop basic agricultural infrastructure along with the keen interest of the villagers.

Growth in North-East India lies in setting up an

institutional framework that is based on sound policies, is governed by clear and transparent rules and regulations and gives local communities a voice in decision-making.[13] If there is declining growth of agriculture in the region, it is because of the fund or credit and the marketing infrastructure. It was mentioned by the then Finance Minister P. Chidambaram that 'Money is not a problem'. India and other countries founded World Bank. World Bank is there to borrow money from it. If not India and other founder countries, who will borrow from it? There is no problem in borrowing money from the World Bank as long as it is used wisely and efficiently without leakages and to create assets and the money is repaid. It is same in the case of this village also. So many institutions whether it is government or non-governmental organizations, are there to provide credit and other facilities, provided it is judiciously utilized or repaid on time. To develop agrarian hill economy, the above facilities should be made available to the real tiller of the land not the leader of the village. It enables the farmers to enhance their productivity and holding capacity to sell their produce at remunerative prices, provided the marketing facilities are made available.

For harnessing the opportunities discussed above, the researcher has identified three policies, which suit the environment of hill economy particularly in Maram Khullen. These are : One, *Production by Masses*; Two, *Contract Farming*; and Three, *Expansion of Technology*.

The first and foremost important policy for materializing the opportunities available in Maram Khullen is *Production by Masses* (see, Swaminathan 2006). It means cultivation of the productive crop, which suits the soil of the region by many farmers at the same time. It helps in capturing market at the economies of scale, provided marketing infrastructure is given by the government. As the cultivators do not produce much more than the subsistence level, the total produce is meagre and is unable to cater to the market demand.

However, if all (or many) cultivators start producing the abundantly growing food crops at the same time in larger quantities, then a constant supply of the produce can be made which will ensure a good profit. Hence, priority should be given to the 'production by masses' category of farming. For this to become a reality, the involvement of the entire community is a must. Priority should be given to mitigation of the problems faced by the cultivators in marketing their small surplus produce. Marketing becomes economically viable only when a constant supply of the produce can be created. Hence, the *'Production by Masses'* type of farming assumes greater significance in these hill tribal villages. When the cultivators start producing a particular crop simultaneously, the advantage due to economies of scale can be realized. If every body in the village (Maram Khullen) produces the productive crops like potato, passion fruit, and squash etc. at the same time, they can create a bigger market supply. But, it should be accompanied by a set of physical infrastructure, like transport and communication, credit facilities, cold storage, proper market linkages etc.

Secondly, *Contract Farming* (see, Phougat 2006) is also equally important for the development of agriculture in the hill villages particularly in Maram Khullen. It signifies a firm or an investor taking the whole responsibilities of investment and marketing of the produce. This arrangement gives security to the poor farmers as regards crop failure, market failures, etc. Since, the cultivators, on their own do not produce surplus goods because of the inhibiting transportation and marketing costs, a pre-production arrangement for sale between the farmers and private firms, processing units, etc., can be made. This type of agribusiness model in the lines of 'contract farming' would be beneficial to the cultivators in the matter of access to adequate or timely credit, good quality inputs, new technology, employment generation, separation of production and marketing risks, better farm practices, etc. The essence of such an arrangement is the commitment of the cultivator to provide an agricultural commodity of a certain type, at a time and a price, and in the quantity required by a known and committed buyer. Here, the farmer would grow the contractor's crop on his land, harvest and deliver to the contractor a quantum of the produce, based upon anticipated yield and contracted acreage. This would be at a pre-agreed price and the contractor assumes all the risks of marketing the produce. But it needs sincerity on the part of farmers in supplying quality, quantity and timely. But, the cultivators of this village lack little interest in this sector due to low income generation and more physical labour is needed in this sector. Perhaps this may be the reason why Passion fruit farm funded by IFAD is not improving in Maram Khullen.

If cultivators are sincere enough, this kind of arrangement is one of the best means to create marketable surplus particularly in Maram Khullen. Contract Farming System is successfully working in many parts of the country. By entering *'Pepsico'* in contract farming in Punjab, the average yield of the contract farmers' is 25-50 per cent higher than the State average, while their per hectare income is reported to be 40 per cent higher than that of other farmers. Normally, poor farmers in the village do not accept any new policy or method easily because they do not want to take risk. So, the contract farming system removes the risk taking part of the poor farmers.

Thirdly, the *Expansion of Technology* (see, e.g., Beardsley *et al.* 1959; Radwan and Lee 1986) is also one of the most essential components in developing agricultural sector. It is nothing but a *vertical expansion* (*Op. cit:* p. 2), which means increasing productivity of land under the cultivation through technical progress. It deals with the impact of technology and agro-infrastructure in developing agriculture. The superstitious belief of the tribal villagers as regards to the practice of double cropping should be removed by educating the villagers about its benefits. Also, methods of improving soil health through integrated nutrient supply by using fertilizers have to be encouraged. The quantum of agricultural output in the village (Maram Khullen) can be multiplied by applying new improved seeds and other mechanical methods including double cropping system. The vast paddy field is free right after harvesting till next monsoon arrives. Only one tractor is available in the village and it is also absolutely free in the off-season (during winter). So, there are number of ways to create marketable surplus of this sector in this village.

There is no dearth of credit advancing agencies for the cultivators but most of the villagers are not aware of it. The few who are aware and avail themselves of loans through these agencies have the tendency of misusing the credit or not repaying it on time. They use credits for unproductive activities, like marriage, domestic consumption purposes, etc. This discourages the financing institutions in providing necessary credit and other financial assistance to the cultivators. The villagers should be made aware of the various credit advancing agencies and the need for repaying the loans timely.

Without a positive economic environment, agricultural growth is impossible. The challenges found in the North-east are, in many ways different those prevalent in other parts of the country. The strategic models or road map towards developing the agricultural sector should be region-specific. Agriculture in the hill villages of North-east with its unique problems needs a comprehensive road map in order to tap its vast potentials. The failure to chart out a North-East-specific agricultural policy has led to the arrested development of agriculture in the hill tribal villages of this region and the perpetuation of poverty in general. The situation is more or less same in this village also. The potential and vast cultivable area of this village is to be utilised in a proper manner.

NOTES & REFERENCES

1. *Jhum* cycle means the period of jhum land left after using 2-3 years in succession for rejuvenation of the land.
2. For hill tribes of NE particularly in Manipur they cannot sell land to other tribes or villages.
3. It means Bachelor's dormitory, built by any of well to do family in the village generally in a clan. It is a tradition for Maram Khullen that clan chief has to build a Morung and it is a pride for them. In the Morung, there is a fire place in the middle squired by four logs of wood used as seats. There are two long beds on both sides of the fire place made of single plunk/ wood each. It can accommodate minimum of 13 to 16 persons and open forever for male members. Fire wood is provided by the Morung owner. Womenfolk are not allowed to sit or sleep on the bed of the Morung. But now-a-days it is used very occasionally during the feast in the village. It is the literal meaning of the term Morung in Maram. In another usage of the term 'Morung land' signifies a land owned by members of a particular Morung of a clan. Here, it is to be noted that a clan may have four or five Morungs depending on the number of people of a clan. The greater the number of people of a clan the greater is the number of Morungs. The members of the Morung are from the same clan but the use of the Morung is open to every one.
4. In the hill villages particularly in Manipur there is no standard of measure of land and in case of Maram Khullen one A*lupak* is a plot of land (wet rice cultivation) in one particular area owned by a family. No matter the size of the land and it should be in a single stretch, not mixing with other's plot in between. If a parent has two sons the plot is to be divided equally into two, each of the plots is also called one *Alupak.*
5. *Jhum* cultivation is no longer in practice now in Maram Khullen because there is no more virgin forest in Maram Khullen area at present. Its main production is rice and productivity level is very low. On the other hand, the village has self-sufficiency in rice production from wet field.
6. If any animal is killed by spear, it is considered as brave and he is honoured for it. As a respect of it, no tax is imposed on him for hunting in other individual's forest.

7. Very recently, Power Tiller and livestock have been introduced for ploughing in the wet rice paddy field.
8. It is a local name of particular hill owned by clans, meant for potato cultivation for market purposes.
9. It is a medium in height (3-5.5 m), half-woody, fast growing and shallow rooted. The long stalked pendent fruit borne singly or in clusters of 3-12 is smooth, egg-shaped but pointed at both sides.
10. As informed by IFAD office, Senapati Headquarters, Manipur.
11. *Op cit*: p.3.
12. See more detail from "The World Bank in India', November 2006 : 3.
13. *Ibid.*

3

Forest, Water and Environment

The study of hill village economy without discussing natural resources would always be incomplete. This chapter discusses the nature and condition of natural resources of Maram Khullen. It includes mainly forest resources, water and environmental condition of the village. The development of a region mainly depends on the availability of the natural resources and efficient utilization of it. According to Irving Fisher, "The under-developed countries, embarking on programmes of economic development usually have to begin with and concentrate on the development of locally available natural resources as an initial condition for lifting local levels of living and purchasing power, for obtaining foreign exchange with which to purchase capital equipment and for setting motion the development process." In this chapter, it is going to study how far the forest and environment, and the water resources influence in the development of hill village economy (Maram Khullen).

Forest Resources

Tribal and forest has a symbiotic relationship since time immemorial. Tribal life, culture and economy intertwine around the forest. If the forest is not there, they might have been called by some other nomenclature, not tribal; probably because of the forest they are called tribal. Forest supplies not only timber, fuel wood and other fruit and vegetables, but also gives life support and green environment. Its proper use can determine the very foundation of a people's economic structure in the village.

The National Forest Policy 1998 Govt. of India envisages people's involvement in the development and protection of forests. It is one of the essentials of forest management that the forest communities should be motivated to identify themselves with development and protection of forests from which they derived benefits. People's involvement in forest management includes four levels. They are :

(i) Participation in planning and decision-making,
(ii) Participation in implementation of projects,
(iii) Participation in monitoring and evaluation, and
(iv) Participation in sharing benefits.

The Government of Manipur by notification has issued constitution of Forest Development Agencies (FDA) in all the Forest Divisions of Manipur including one FDA in the wild-life wing of the Forest Department. The Govt. of Manipur has also constituted Joint Forest Management Committees (JFMCs) to participate in regeneration, protection, conservation and management of degraded forests inclusive of un-classed forests. The main concern and thrust of FDA project implemented through various registered JFMCs are tree planting, soil and moisture conservation, awareness campaign providing various socio-economic development activities to the village communities through Entry Point Activities (EPA), Monitoring and Evaluation, etc.

Manipur has 78.01 per cent of its total geographical area covered by forests in 2002-03 according to the office of the Principal Chief Conservator of Forest, Manipur. This accounts for an area of 17,418 sq. km. under forest cover. The legal position of the forest administration in the State is fluid, which means there is no blueprint division on the control over the forest. The government has extended its control to a small portion of the forest comprising of 1,467 sq. km. of Reserved Forest and 4,171 sq. km. of Protected Forest which together constitute only 25.25 per cent of the total area or 31.99 per cent of the total forest area. The remaining 68.01 per cent of forests are unclassified forests under the control of the tribal populations. These unclosed forests are subject to widespread injudicious exploitation of the hill people who at some area meticulously guard patches of tree growth.

Forest Resources in Maram Khullen

Like agricultural land, the prevailing forest land tenure of Maram Khullen is classified into four types. Those are : (1) Individual forest land, (2) Morung forest land[1], (3) Clan forest land, and (4) Village forest land. Around three-fifth of the total geographical area owned by the village is forest land (all four types together). Practically, there is no dense forest or virgin forest as such in the village now. If there is any unsettled disputed individual forest land, transfers to the Morung to which the land belongs. Again if it is not settled in the Morung, goes to clan and even to the village in a hierarchical manner. Roughly, out of the total forest area of the village, Clan forest land occupies highest proportion at 35 per cent followed by Individual forest land (30 per cent), Village forest land (25 per cent) and Morung forest land (10 per cent). Both the Individual and the Morung forest land produce mainly fire-wood for self-consumption. The Clan and the Village forest land produce fire-wood and little timber, which is used for commercial purposes occasionally when the community requires some for community's development programme.

Table 3.1 : Rough Area of Forest and its Produces

Type of ownership		*Per cent*	*Main Produces*	*Purpose*
Individual	forest land	30	Fire-wood	Self-consumption
Morung	forest land	10	Fire-wood	Self-consumption
Clan	forest land	35	Fire-wood & Timber	For Self-consumption and Market
Village	forest land	25	Fire-wood & Timber	For Self-consumption and Market

Source : Survey.

In Maram Khullen, almost all (approximately 95 per cent) the family uses fire-wood for cooking and other domestic fuel purposes. The forest in the village gives sufficient fire-wood for self-consumption, even if it cannot produce surplus for commercial purposes. Those families, who do not have their individual forest land, could use other's forest for collecting fire-wood by giving 50 per cent of fire-wood as loyalty to the owner. In other way, one can get fire-wood for self-consumption from other's forest by paying his/her labour in other mutually agreed form to the owner of the forest. Geographically, the Village forest land is the farthest forest land from the village and this land has the highest timber potentials for commercial purposes. It is because of its land-lock location, from which the timbers cannot be brought out to the road side easily. Individual forest land mainly produces fire-wood for self-consumption. Morung forest also produces fire-wood for consumption of the Morung members and for commercial purposes as well. Clan and Village forest land give fire-wood as well as timber for both purposes.

When community's land is decided upon commercial activities, the land is leased out to the traders[2] whether it may be Morung, Clan or Village forest land. The lease may be normally for one to five years. During this period, the lessee can extract as much resources as he can. The amount received from the lease is used for common purposes. For instance, the amount is usually utilised for the annual community's feast and certain amount is distributed among the old aged, the poor and the handicaps of the community.

Though this business is not regular, the average annual income (benefit according to the price of 2006) of the traders is estimated to be around rupees one lakh. The number of traders for the forests of Maram Khullen is around 5 to 6. They normally do not cut the fire-wood or timber during the rainy season because the cut fire-wood or timber gets rotten very fast during the rainy season. Buffalo is used for transporting these timber and fire-wood from hill top to road side. Despite having handsome profit in this business say approximately Rs. 1-2 lakh annually depending on the size of the forest, people cannot rush in this business easily now due to formal ban from the government on one hand and heavy taxes from the unauthorized agencies (underground groups) on the other.

The analysis in this section is that, the environment and the economic development have negative co-relationship between them. The development of an economy leads to at least some destruction of environment. Here, the question is, can we get both? If we get both, how do we manage it? This is known by the term 'Sustainable Development' by the Environmental Economists. Sustainable development is in the threat in the village because of the fact that cutting down trees is not followed up by tree plantation. On account of this very practice, people of the village and the surrounding areas have started to feel the shortage of water more seriously than it had been earlier. Another impact of this is the realisation of the people in the rise of temperature even during the winter season.

Table 3.2 : Size of the Forest land owned in Maram Khullen (in terms of *Abang*[3])

Size of Forest land owned	*No. of Household*	*Percentage of household*
0	52	12.03
1	81	18.75
2	128	29.62
3	124	28.70
4	43	9.95
5	4	0.92
Total	**432**	**100**

Source : Survey.

Water Resource

For leading to a healthy and hygienic life, there is a minimum water requirement in a day. It varies according to places and the living standards of the people. As per the Bureau of Indian Standards, IS : 1172-1993, a minimum water supply of 200 litres per capita per day (lpcd) should be provided for domestic consumption in cities with full flushing systems. Further it mentions that the amount of water supply may be reduced to 135 lpcd for the low income group and the economically weaker sections of the society and in small towns. The National Commission on Urbanization (1988) recommended that per capita water supply of 90-100 litres per day is needed to lead a hygienic existence, and emphasized that this level of water supply must be ensured to all citizens. Compared internationally, domestic water consumption in Munich is 130 lpcd, in Amsterdam it is 156 lpcd and in Singapore it is 162 lpcd. International norms set out by agencies such as World Health Organization (WHO) and the United Nations International Children's Emergency Fund (UNICEF) suggest a minimum requirement of 20 litres a day from a source within one kilometre of the household. This is sufficient for drinking and basic personal hygiene (HDR 2006).

Table 3.3 : Minimum Water Requirement (Per Capita per Day)

UNICEF	**NCU (with full Flushing System)*
20 Litres	90-100 Litres

Source : Compiled from *UNews*, July (2006) and HRD (2006).

* National Commission on Urbanization.

It must be noted here that there is no strong basis for this benchmark, but it is a rough average requirement in order to maintain a minimum standard of health and hygiene. In the finding of Shaban and Sharma (2007), in so far as activity-wise consumption of water at the household level is concerned, bathing consumes the highest amount of water (28 per cent), followed by toilets (20 per cent), washing cloths (18.6 per cent) and washing utensils (16.3 per cent). On an average, less than 10 per cent of the total water in a household is used for drinking and cooking.

Table 3.4 : Activity-wise consumption of Water

(in Per cent)

Bathing	*Toilet*	*Washing Cloth*	*Washing Utensil*	*Drinking and Cooking*
28	20	18.6	16.3	8.1

Source : Shaban and Sharma (2007).

Water Stress in Maram Khullen

The village faces acute drinking water problem starting from the off season of November till March. People do really understand the essence and the nectar of the water in these months, and the most sufferers of the problem are the womenfolk. Vagaries of monsoon, like late onset, early withdrawal prolonged dry spell etc. have added to the problem. The peak of this resource scarcity on which life runs on, is during the month of December to February. During this period, not to exaggerate, no woman is found leisuring or engaging oneself on something else. Womenfolk ranging from the age of 4 years to 80s are seen with a jar (*Akii*) in their basket (*Arak*) on their backs all day through. This hectic daily job does not end here, as the sun sets, we witness people once again in a row with torches in their hands towards water sources, some proceeding to draw, others withdrawing; this is still worst in moon lid nights. In fact there is no time of the day when one will not witness this movement of womenfolk during this scarcity period as the ants do on a sunny day for their food. It is noteworthy that this hunt for water is basically for cooking. In addition to this problem is the notable duration of time taken to fill a jar from the dying, dripping droplets between hillocks and gorges. As for bathing, washing and other usages of water, people in this village have to walk miles. No wonder then that when such acute drinking water scarcity is being experienced, sanitation becomes casualty. Our primary village survey gives a rough estimation of 14 litres lpcd available in average in the village.

Earlier Attempt

The Government of Manipur sometimes in 1980s undertook a project to supply water from a gorge source called '*Lakshe Maidui*' about 4 km from the village. A reservoir was built, pipe line laid, a water motor pump was installed at the source. When a day before the operation of the project could start, the motor pump was stolen, believed to be secretly sold out by the engineer-cum-contractor of the project. Despite heavy investment and labour incurred in the said project, no motor pump was replaced, which led to utter failure of the project. A year following this incident, the Assam rifle camped at Maram Bazaar had collected the pipes for their use with some payment of cash as a consolation for the failure of the project to the village authority.

Table 3.5 : Population and Water availability in Maram Khullen

Total Household	*Total Population*	*Average Family size*	*Water per head*
432	2374	5.5	14 litres

Source : Field Survey.

A decade later, in 1992 with the initiative of the constituency candidate (Ex-MLA) Late Ng. Luikang, the government engineered rain water harvesting project and installed ordinary hand pumps in the village as an alternative to the project's failure of 1980s. As a result of it, 7 hand pumps were installed and 4 tanks were built. But only 2 hand pumps could draw water effectively. Unfortunately, these hand pump's water could neither be used for cooking nor for washing as the water contained strong arsenic contamination, strong intoxication, irritating odour and coloured creamy muddy. To the dismay of the people, the tank did no better good as it withered, holed-patches, as the tank was thinly walled which was a picturesque sight a tank built, fulfilling no purpose as a reservoir.

Table 3.6 : Water Source and Scarcity period in the Village

Scarcity period	*Source of Water*	*Distance during rainy season*	*Distance during off season*
January - March	Perennial Hillock	$^1/_2$ km	4 km

Source : Survey.

Present Attempt

Today (at the time of survey in September 2006), with the coming up of an international Non-Governmental Organization (NGO), named International Fund for

Agricultural Development (IFAD) with its regional head-quarter in Shillong is undertaking a water supply project in the village. The project tries to tap water from a very reliable source place called *'Ragong'* towards the north 4 km away from the village. With the contribution of 22 Self-Help Groups (SHGs) of Rs. 10,000 (Ten thousands) each (total of Rs. 2,20,000) the NGO is on the process of pipe lining, finishing 3 km at the time of field survey was conducted.

Clean water and sanitation are among the most powerful drivers for human development. They extend opportunity, enhance dignity and help to create a virtuous cycle of improving health and rising wealth (HDR 2006). The direct result of water crisis in the village is poor health and lost of productive time and, indirectly affecting the economy.

Water is a social good, so every citizen has the right to have it. It is a legitimate duty of the government in making it available to each and very citizen of the country. But the effective maintenance and proper distribution of water lies in the hands of consumers. It is the duty of the consumers not only to ensure that their rights are safeguarded but to work with the government in implementing the right. (see, Pangare and Pangare 2007). Prime Minister, Dr. Manmohan Singh said : 'We should move forward, move towards forging a partnership between the government and citizens for conserving water'. There has been a substantial enhancement in the allocation from Rs. 4,560 crores during 2006-07 to Rs. 6,500 crores during the current financial year for rural drinking water supply schemes. Further, he said the onus now is on the State government to ensure that these resources get translated into actual entitlement of safe drinking water and improve services for the benefit of common man.

Now here comes the questions; what are the root causes of water problem in the tribal villages? In the rainy season there comes surplus or flood, struggling for the control but in the off season every drop of it counts and it is very precious. More than two-third of the earth is water and less than one per cent of it is oil but oil can be had anywhere in as much quantity as we like. What explains the difference? Water is a free-open access resource; oil is not free, it is owned and managed. It is not like a Zero-sum game in which one gets less if others get more. As the society develops, the need of water is also increasing day by day. All the developed countries are getting safe and sufficient drinking water. The only poor countries are facing water problem. Field studies by the Nicaraguan Centre for Studies and Action for Development showed that, the presence of water for household use and horticulture (on properties of less than 7 hectares) can raise income by as much as a third. This water crisis is largely of our own making. It is not because nature has not provided enough water or for lack of financing and appropriate technologies, even though these are important factors but rather from failures in water governance, that would clarify who gets how much water, when and how to decide who has the right to water and related services (*UNews*, July 2006).

One important thing to note here is that, the quantity of water consumption in this village is not determined by the demand of the consumers but the level of quantity available in the village. Poor villagers try to manage the water according to the available supply without any extra effort.

Argument of Water Problem in the Village

According to Dinesh Chand[4], Agro-Climatic Zones and Drinking Water availability are demarcated into 16 Zones. In which large areas of Sikkim, Manipur, Darjeeling-hills, Arunachal Pradesh, Meghalaya, Nagaland, Assam, Mizoram, Jalpaiguri and Cooch Behar of West Bengal are categorized as humid high rainfall North-Eastern Zone. Nevertheless, almost all the hill villages in the NE are facing shortage of water for human consumption, whereas it is not so much in the towns and the cities comparatively. Why do not they (the city dwellers and rich people) have that intense water problem as the hill villagers in the NE face? Could the reasons be on account of poverty, half-hearted attention of the consumers, government's negligence or the absence of funding agencies for proper implementation of infrastructures for water supply?

Everyone feels water shortage in the hill villages, particularly the village of Maram Khullen in Manipur. The primary village survey reveals the fact that the availability of water in the village is only 14 lcpd, which is much lower than the standard norm of 20 lpcd set by the international agencies. In Maram Khullen, major share of available water in the village is used for cooking and drinking. Bathing and toilet consume least water because majority of the household uses *Katcha* latrine. This could be one of the reasons why, around 20 per cent of the households have migrated in this decade towards the highway (NH 39), for easy access to water supply and other conveniences too. Why cannot we solve this water problem in Maram Khullen when others could get adequately? For instance, the institution of Don Bosco at Maram centre (on the foothill of Maram Khullen), which consists of Higher Secondary School, College and other vocational courses offered by the institution could avail themselves of the ample supply of the resource. The institution (School, Higher Secondary and College together) has about 2000 students in addition to the number of workers and the staff there, who sufficiently receive the required water consumption need. Similarly, the Assam Rifle camped at Maram Bazaar, which is also on the foothill of the village, numbering around 1500 people do receive water supply sufficiently. The former gets water from the source, that flows down the village foothill and the latter receives from the source of a small stream at the foothill of Maram Khullen.

Now a question that arises is if the two institutions are in the position to have sustainability of ample drinking water, why not this village? Maram Khullen too should be able to receive the same. Then what could be the stumbling block that has made able to the supply of the adequate water resource to Maram Khullen? We can in general accept the fact that, the reason behind the resource scarcity, to that of the half hearted attention of the government towards the needs of the people within its jurisdiction, the lack of initiative, interests and the ignorance along with the people's negligence facilitating the elite group to warm up their pockets rather than fulfil people's need, have added to the seriousness of the problem.

Why the villagers cannot nap the culprit, who stole the water pipe and punished the engineer who constructed the thinly walled water reservoir in the village? The village could have reported the government right after the incident or they could have demanded for an alternative project in place of the failed project. It is not difficult for a tribal village to nap such culprits because the village laws are more firm and stringent than the State. On the other hand, the common tragedy we find in the public sector projects are often than not 'a failure'. Projects are implemented for the sake of project without any proper policy and there is no follow up system after the implementation of the project, particularly in the hill villages. Institutions continue to function in a top-down manner. The need of the hour is not only the development of water resources but also their efficient management in a sustainable manner. According to Pangare and Pangare (2007),[5] 'It is important to first recognize that access to water and sanitation is nothing to be granted as a commodity or in charity. Access to water and sanitation is the right of every citizen and therefore must be provided and safeguarded by the State. Awareness must be created in the people and the government regarding the meaning of the right to water and the obligation that the right imposes on the government'.

Some Suggestions

Given the importance of water crisis, the management of

water resources is one of the most important tasks in the hill villages now. *'Swajaldhara'* is a project for providing safe drinking water in the rural areas. The communities have to contribute 5 per cent of the estimated capital cost of the project in case of predominantly Scheduled Tribe/ Scheduled Caste habitations as per 2001 census and the remaining 95 per cent is funded by the Central Government. This contribution of community is purposely designed so as to make the village community feel themselves as part and parcel of the scheme; otherwise the government could have funded the entire cost as well. It is the most important policy in government funded projects. The scheme can never be a success, in the absence of the community's participation. The follow up of the scheme by the government in co-ordination of the villagers is of prime importance for the sustenance of the Scheme. Another project *'Swajal'*, a pilot project for the government of Uttar Pradesh and Uttarakhand supported by the World Bank in the 1990s, became the model for the government of India's Rural Water Supply and Sanitation Programme (RWSS). The project broke the past practices by involving villagers in the planning, construction and operation of their water delivery systems.[6]

In the context of proper maintenance of project, the mobilization of materials and the financial resources to meet the day to day expenses like power charges, chlorine cost, operator charge and other maintenance cost are to be taken cared of seriously. Given the importance of the above statement; who will bear these running costs for its proper operation. An answer to this question is that the running cost of the scheme can be fully borne by the community through user-charges. According to Michael Camdessus[7], the financing of water must obey the principle 'you use it, you pay for it'. Next, the vital question here is, who will run the scheme? Majority of the water problems are the result of the 'Tragedy of the Commons' as Hardin (1968) termed it in environmental issues. Once it sets on target the project will function smoothly if the ownership among them is sustained because the community pays the price for it.

Another means of mitigating the water crisis in the hill villages is the rain water harvesting system, which is technically simple and financially viable in the poor region. More than 90 per cent of the houses in Maram Khullen are tin roof (CI sheets) but no family adopts rain water harvesting system in the village. Simple concrete tanks to collect rain water during rainy season can be of a great help to the problem during its acute period. Studies have revealed the fact that rooftop rainwater harvesting could meet over 60 per cent of domestic needs and prevent soil erosion.

The significance of the very concept of the community based participation for providing safe drinking water and their direct involvement in the equitable distribution of the resource supply scheme has not been taken seriously in the hill tribal villages in the North East India, particularly in Maram Khullen. The need of the hour is, to create awareness among the people of the indispensable need of water for living a hygienic life. This calls for people's active participation and co-operation in co-ordination with the government. Another important factor is, to set up a committee to supervise the management to ensure proper maintenance and distribution of water. The committee is to appoint a caretaker, for smooth functioning of the scheme or project.

In the process of transmission of water supply, a strong political will of the government to frame appropriate water policies, with the co-operation of the consumers along with the indomitable conscience of the villagers specially the womenfolk to utilize water judiciously is absolutely a necessity, for adequate drinking water sustainability. Women have an important role to play in the development of water management and sustainability. The 4th UN World Conference on Women[8] recognizes the importance of women in natural resources management emphasized the active involvement of women in development making process of management. Here, the gender bias should go and the village local bodies should not have women member for namesake to fulfil constitutional obligation but to play an effective role to manage water resources in a judicious and equitable manner as they bear the major responsibility of household activities of the family. For this village, long term policy perspective is to be framed with the support of community. Water is one of the most important components in our life. So, it is to be given special priority and harnessed in a sustainable way.

NOTES & REFERENCES

1. Land owned by the members of the Morung.
2. When community's land is decided upon commercial activities, any one could take up the contract for generating income based on the consensus of both the parties.
3. It is a plot of forest land owned by an individual or a group of people from where fire-woods for domestic purpose are procured. The size of an *Abang* is same as interpreted in an *Alupak* in the previous chapter.
4. Additional Advisor, Department of Drinking Water Supply, Ministry of Rural Development, New Delhi.
5. Pangare, V. and Pangare, G. (2007); Inplementing the Rights to Water, New Delhi : *Yojana* Vol. 51 (Sept.) p. 9
6. The World Bank in India, Jan. 2007.
7. Former Director General, International Monetary Fund.
7. The 4th UN World Conference on Women was held in Beijing in 1995.

4

Education, Health and Population

This chapter deals with some of the social sectors like education, health and population which are the basic constituents of a society. The role of these sectors so-called social variables in fostering economic progress has recently received much attention in the development literature (Dreze and Sen 1996 :13). The development of these sectors helps directly or indirectly in determining development of a village or an economy. Development does not signify only the growth of output or production in an economy; it includes structural or institutional changes in a society. In this regard, some selected social sectors are discussed below:

Education

In the study of Porter (2000) found that the association between human capital and economic well-being is derived from the early work of T. W. Schultz. Porter's research further suggested that economic growth is largely the result of investments in human capital. Again he argued that increases in the capital-income ratio are largely due to human capital development, not material capital, which was originally thought to account for all increases in income and subsequent economic growth. He further suggested that investments in human knowledge and skill are the critical determinants of economic growth and are necessary if regions lacking human capabilities ever expect to attract and fully benefit from infusions of new capital. High performance work practices rely on skilled workers. No matter how powerful the computer hardware or how user-friendly the software, most functions provided by computers still require hands-on human contact to be productive (Gordon 2000 : 49-74). It is the ability to effectively use the advances of technology that will determine which communities will flourish and which will be left behind. Communities that are able to train and/or attract a technologically competent labour force will be better able to attract and retain globally competitive firms.

Developing societies/countries require a rapid qualitative growth and higher education for their very survival in the highly competitive world. In the findings of Tilak (2005), only those nations having high ratio of enrolment in higher education (say about 20 per cent) could become economically advanced and vice versa. Quality education (not quantity) is the only real asset and inevitable capital for sustainable development in a society. It is being advocated that global wealth today is concentrated less in factories and machinery that knowledge and skills are increasingly becoming critical to the world economy (D'Souza 2004).

Christian Missionaries and Education in the Village

Though it is bit late, Maram Khullen is catching up global education very fast after introducing Christian Missionary education system. It is not exaggerating that, the light of education in this village is given by the Christian Missionaries. Almost all the educated youths of Maram Khullen village are the blessings of these institutions. We have to thank specially them for imparting English education (which is the most important education system in this modern competitive world) to the tribal people and this village in particular. In the words of B. M. Pugh[1], 'The tribes of NE India today feel greatly indebted to the Missionaries of the West for their work of uplifting them'. Barpujari (2004) argues that if the Missionaries would not have come to the rescue of the British administration by taking over the charge of the education of the tribes, the progress of education which was slow in the hills would have been slower still, it would not have an exaggeration to say that Christianity and education developed in the hills of the North-East like twin sisters.

Table 4.1 : Qualification-wise distribution of the Population in Maram Khullen

Educational Qualification	*Number*	*Per cent to the total population*
Above Post Graduate	1 (M. Phil.)	0.04
Post Graduate	17	0.71
Graduate	89	3.4
XII standard	120	5.05
X standard	265	11.16
Only read and write only	719	30.27
Illiterate	761	32.02
Under schooling age	404	17
Total	2376	100

Source : Survey.

Educational Level in the Village

Despite being concerted efforts to uplift educational level in the village by Christian Missionary Institutions, the literacy rate is quite low (see Table 4.1), it is approximately 51 per cent compared to the State (68.87 per cent in 2001 census) and educated persons (Matriculate and above) is 20.36 per cent. The major increase in student's enrolment was in the colleges of general education, whereas there was a negligible increase in the science and commerce education. The enrolment in the Technical and Management education is absolutely zero till the field survey was conducted. Even if there are some considerable increases in the enrolment into the higher education, majority of them got enrolled in the theory type papers.

Table 4.2 : No. of Persons in Higher Education and Employment in the Village

Stream	*Level of Education and No.*		*No. of Employment**
1. Arts	Graduate	75	7
	Post Graduate	12	6
2. Science	Graduate	8	Nil
	Post Graduate	6	4
3. Commerce	Graduate	5	1
	Post Graduate	Nil	Nil
4. Medical	Graduate	1	1
	Post Graduate	Nil	Nil
5. Technical	Graduate	Nil	Nil
	Post Graduate	Nil	Nil
6. Management	Graduate	Nil	Nil
	Post Graduate	Nil	Nil
Total	Sl. No. 1-6	**107**	**19**

Source : Field Survey.

* Including employment in the Private Sector.

From Table 4.2 it is clear that the graduate in Science and Arts are 8 and 75 respectively. In the case of post graduate, this village has 6 and 12 in Science and Arts respectively. It is comparatively very high in a tribal village and more importantly in a primitive tribal community. This clearly shows that the village is comparatively much better than any other PTGs in the country due to the Missionary institutions.

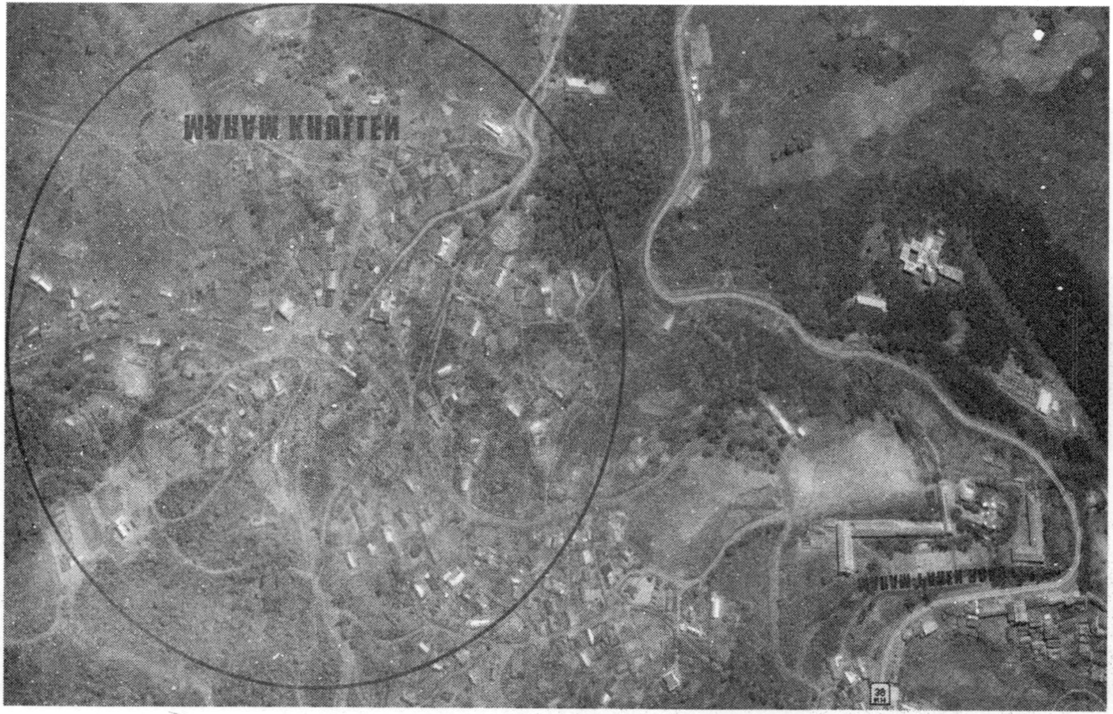

Photo 1.1 : Google Earth Photo of Maram Khullen.

Photo 2.1 : Tilling with the help of Buffalo and Wooden Plough (A demonstration).

Photo 2.2 : Squash/Biscoti.

Photo 2.3 : Type of Cabbage available in Maram Khullen.

Photo 2.4 : Tree Tomato

Photo 2.5 : River-bed Paddy Field.

Photo 2.6 : Terrace Cultivation Field.

Photo 2.4 : Some Agricultural Implements

Photo 2.8 : Basket/*Arak*, Granary.

Photo 4.1 : 1. Don Bosco College. 2. John Paul II School.

Photo 4.2 : Govt. School in the Village.

Photo 4.3 : Public Health Centre and Veterinary Centre.

Photo 4.4 : Kitchen of a Maram Family.

Photo 7.1 : Queen at Her Residence.

Photo 7.2 : Morung (Bachelors' Dormitory) and Morung Door.

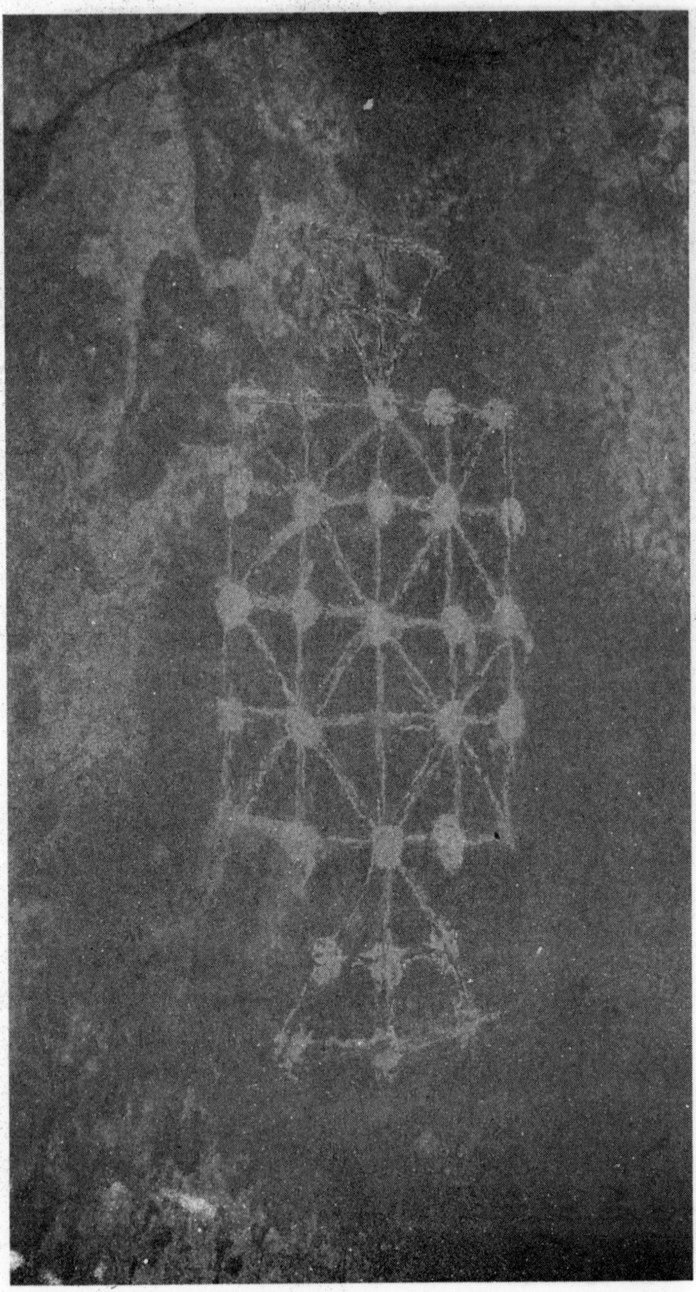

Photo 7.3 : Type of Game in the Village .

Educational Infrastructures

Educational infrastructures are concerned in the Maram Khullen, there is a Government Junior High School established in 1967[2] with classes up to VIII standard and one private school, John Paul II established in 1986 (with classes from Nursery to VII standard) run by Catholic Missionary. Apart from these, for high school and higher secondary level, there is a school named 'Don Bosco Higher Secondary School' (in higher secondary level offers only Science stream) and for higher studies, Don Bosco College (both Secondary level and Under-graduate level offering subjects of Science, Arts & Commerce) are just below the foothill of the village. Both these were established in the year 1982 and 2000 respectively (see photo 4.1).

While, the Government Junior School is practically not functioning now (see photo 4.2). No teacher and student were found in the school at the time of survey visit in the village. No villager can reveal properly who are the teachers in this school. Whereas, the Mission school is the only school functioning smoothly and providing proper education in the village.

Table 4.3 : Population, Education and Employment in the Village

Total Population	*No. of Matriculates and above (Educated Persons)*	*% of Population attained Higher Education**	*% of Higher educated persons employed***
2376	265	40.38	17.76

Source : Field Survey.

* Calculated from the No. of Matriculates in the village.

** Calculated from the No. of persons attained Higher education and employment including Private Sector.

Table 4.3 reveals that the employment rate who attained higher education is 17.76 per cent only. The total number of population attained higher education (Degree and above) level is 107 persons out of total 265 educated persons (Matriculate and above) i.e. 40.38 per cent. And the number of the educated persons in the village is 265 persons (Matriculate and above), it is approximately 11.15 per cent of the total population.

Analysis of the Data

In the analysis of educational data of this village, it has some fillip and flop points. To start with the fillip side, this village has some advantages of having one of the best institutions in the State.[3] Though they have established lately, these institutions have shown the light of education to this village. The light of education has come to this village from the 1980s. Secondly, English is the medium of instruction in these institutions, which is one of the most important factors for attaining higher education and for getting employment in this globalization era. Thirdly, the post-matric scholarship[4] is also one of the stepping stones for pursuing higher education in the village. Higher education is the prime factor for a society to compete with the challenges brought about by the globalization. Scholars (like, Tilak 2005 and others) have argued that the threshold level of gross enrolment ratio in higher education is about 20 per cent, which the Maram Khullen has already crossed. Only those countries that could have such a ratio could become economically advanced.

On the flop side, despite the available infrastructures, the drop-out rate before reaching class X standard is quite high; say approximately 25 to 30 per cent. Secondly, the employability (human capital) rate, which can compete in the global market, is also quite low (see Table 4.3). About 17.76 per cent only are employed (including the private farms) out of the total population attained higher education.[5] The basic cause is attributed to the few factors listed below.

First, the Government Junior High School in the village is not functioning at present. Second, the education imparted by the private agent is very expensive. Third, there is no system of pre-matric scholarship; so elementary education became very expensive (since only private school is working). Poor parents who are living on subsistence agriculture cannot afford the expenses of private education. Private schools are very much strict with uniform, textbooks and other stationery items which cannot be afforded easily by the poor parents in the village. Scholars (like, Tilak 2005; De *et al*. 2002; Shah 2006; Barpujari 1994) argued that the private institutions cannot bring quality and sustainable education in the long run. Last but not the least, there is not much educational inspiration from the part of the parents because of their ignorance and illiteracy. Illiterate parents prefer their children to help them in their cultivation. Moreover, there is not much competition among the villagers.

Population

Usually, the people of this village live in nuclear families. Practically it is not easy to know the exact number of population and households of Maram Khullen. As mentioned in the limitation of the study above, many families of this village have second house on the National Highway (NH 39) or market areas. It has a tendency of the people to migrate to urban areas for easy access of the modern amenities of life. According to Shimray (2003)[6], the total population of Maram tribe as a whole in 1991 was 9,592 and the percentage share of total population of Manipur was only 0.52 per cent. The approximate population[7] of Maram Khullen is around 2,376 at the time of village survey i.e. in the month of September 2006. The sex ratio is 926 per cent per thousand male and the average family size in the village is 6 members. Table 4.4 gives clearly the total population and sex-wise break up of the village calculated from the 202 household samples and the age-wise break up is given in Table 4.5.

Table 4.4 : Village Household and Population

Total Household	*Total Population**	*Male*	*Female*	*Ratio per Thousand*
432	2376	1234	1142	925.4

Source : Survey.

* Approximate population (calculated from 202 households sample survey through average family size 5.5).

The present concern of the study of population is to analyse the impact and influence of population to the village economy. In this regard, conventionally, it can be studied in two different dimensions. On the positive side, it provides human labour essentially needed for economic development and growth. On the negative side, increase in population creates unemployment and shortage of food production. In the words of A. C. Pigou, "Human beings are ends in themselves and factors of production as well". Karl Marx also said, "Without human beings both the capital as well as the machinery was just useless. There is direct correlation between population and economic development till the optimum level (in which the economy gets maximum income per head with the given resources) reaches (Singha 2007)."

During the 19th century, 60 per cent of United States of America's capital formation was on account of population growth. But the argument in this study is slightly different from the conventional one mentioned above. Singha (2007) argues it is not harm if the increase in population is accompanied by a greater increase in output and technology in the economy. Maram Khullen is experiencing population growth moderately and, it does not create any negative impact on economy because the average family size in the village is still 6 members only. The subsistence system of economy is not much disturbed by the slight growth of population in the village. The increased population does not give any pressure on the resources available in the village. In the last 1-2 decades, the increased population (about 25-30 per cent) of the village has migrated to the urban areas.

Table 4.5 : Age-wise Distribution of Population in the Village

Age group (in Years)	*Male*	*Female*	*Total*
Below 5	105	97	202
5-10	203	187	390
11-15	160	148	308
16-25	309	286	595
26-35	167	154	321
36-50	113	105	218
Above 50	178	164	342

Source : Survey.

More than 100 families have migrated to the road side (NH 39) fully or partially[8] for convenience and better water facilities. As income increases or living standard improves (including educational level) in the village, people intend to migrate to market areas. Still many people in the village are in the process to migrate to the urban areas. This is the reason why the socio-economic condition of the village is not much changed. Those well-to-do people who have migrated to urban areas do not have much interest for the development of the village. So, the increase in population does not have much impact on the socio-economic condition of the village.

Health

Health is also one of the most important determinants for

measuring human development index. It reflects the socio-economic condition of a society. The National Health Policy (2002) sets out the basic objective of achieving an acceptable standard of good health amongst the general population of the country. It lays emphasis on providing increased access to decentralized public health system, enhancing public health investment, and convergence of public programmes. The National Common Minimum Programme also placed emphasis on raising public health investment with focus on primary health care and increased investment programmes to control communicable diseases. It envisages an increase in public spending on health to 2-3 per cent of GDP by increased contributions from the Central and State Governments.[9] Poor health in the family results to the reverse process of multiplier income. If a bread earner in the family falls sick, the income process in the family goes back to negative process. So, there is a direct correlation between health condition and economy.

In Maram Khullen, the health and sanitation are very poor which affects directly the village economy. But it is not easy to assess the health condition of a village unless and until special medical test is conducted. For the present study the researcher had to take some assumption on the basis of available medical facilities. So far the physical infrastructure of medical facility is concerned, there is a public health centre in the village but that never opens. The duty in-charge assigned in this health centre is a compounder, Mr. Hingba from Senapati who never comes to the centre. Nobody knows who are among the staff in this centre? If emergency arises, they go to Maram Bazaar where a health centre is there and the doctor in-charge was born in Maram Khullen and migrated down there. Still, if it is a serious case, they usually go to Imphal. Majority of the people in this village practise herbal medicines and traditional medication system. In short, medical facility is almost nil in this village.

Table 4.6 : Type of Toilet in the Village

Type of Latrine	Percent of Family
Katcha	97
Open Field	1.99
Both	1.1
Total	**100**

Source : Field Survey.

The reason for poor health and sanitation in this village can be attributed basically to three factors. First, scarcity of water is one of the most important problems, water borne and other sanitation related diseases are the common diseases in the village. In regard to toilet, about 97 per cent of the families in the village use Katcha latrine. This shows low level of sanitation and it directly affects the health. Scarcity of water is the sign of poor sanitation in the village. Second, negligence of the government is also equally responsible to this problem. There is no intervention of the government in this regard. It makes medical infrastructure very poor for the villagers.

Third, social and cultural factor is also an important in this regard. Almost all the houses[10] in the village are without windows and ventilators. About 98 per cent of the households in this village use firewood and apart from this, all the activities like granary, poultry (rearing duck, chicken and pigeon etc.), poundering paddy, domestication of pet animals (dog, cat etc.) are done inside the house. About 92 per cent of the households have earthen floor and 68.31 per cent have mud and bamboo mixed walls in the village.

The Constitution of India lays down that the State shall regard the rising of the health nutrition and the standard of living of its people and the improvement of public health as among its primary duties. Since public health is a public good, it is one of the most important duties of the State to take initiative for the health services. But where have all gone in this village? On the other hand, it is also the duty of the village to take active role in this regard. It is the grievance of the villagers that they have to take initiatives if the government fails to do the functions.

NOTES & REFERENCES

1. As quoted by Jayaseelan (1996 : 19).
2. As reported by James Karaiba, an educationist of Maram Khullen.
3. Don Bosco College (both Secondary and Under-graduate sections) became one of the best Colleges in the State.
4. All the Scheduled Tribe/Schedule Caste students are given post-matric scholarship for pursuing higher education.
5. It implies graduate and above.
6. Input from : Office of the Registrar General and Census Commissioner, 1991. Special Tables for SC/ST, Series 13, Manipur Part IX, Controller of Publications, Delhi.
7. Officially, the total population of Manipur in 2001 census is excluding 3 Sub-Divisions of Senapati district namely Mao-Maram, Paomata and Purul.
8. Partial migration signifies the families living in both places (Maram Khullen and Urban areas).
9. Economic Survey 2005-06, p. 212.
10. It is because of the tradition system.

5

Globalization and Tribal Village

The present world is the era of globalization, it relates with market. Tomlinson (1999:32) opined, globalization is an empirical condition of the complex connectivity involves overcoming cultural distances through penetrating experiences provided through education, employment, consumer culture and the mass media which had been described as more significant than technological advances and physical mobility. Globalization is an inevitable process, which we cannot escape at all. Whether we like it or not we have to go with it. Though the very institution 'Globalization' became a buzz word very recently after 1990s especially in India, it has been associating with human civilization from the time immemorial. The globalization and the market are the two sides of the same coin. In nutshell, globalization implies the opening of economy to the outside world.

In this chapter, a modest attempt is made to analyse the importance and impact of globalization in Maram Khullen. Whether, the village can face the challenges brought about by the globalization or not is the question that arises before us. What will be the feasible solution to extract maximum utility from the globalization is also discussed in this chapter.

Market and Globalization

Globalization is the process by which whole world becomes a single market. It means that goods and services, capital and labour are traded on a worldwide basis. Robertson and Khondkher (1998) have analyzed the globalization as the process of which the compression of entire world on the one hand and increase in consciousness of the whole world on the other. The Human Development Report (1999) has elaborated that globalization comprises global market, global technology, global ideas and global solidarity. According to Jain (2001:1-10), 'Globalization is understood as an economic idea. It is linked with liberalization. But, at the local level, when globalization comes to a village, it changes a lot. Besides economic changes, there is a cultural change also'. In the words of Bhagwati (2006 : 3), 'Economic globalization constitutes integration of national economies into the international economy through trade; FDI, short-term capital flows, international flows of workers and humanity generally, and flows of technology'.

Origin of Globalization

In the pre-modern period (pre-1500), the key agents of globalization were three-folds (1) Political and Military empires, (2) World religions, and (3) the Migratory movements of Nomadic groups. In the early modern period (1500-1800), the rise of the west was regarded as the key agents of globalization. In the modern period (1850-1945) witness an enormous acceleration in the spread and entrenchment of global networks and flows that had begun in the early modern period. And in the contemporary period from 1950 onwards, globalization was shaped profoundly by the structural consequences of the Second World War and the emergence of a worldwide system of nation States, overlaid by multilateral, regional and global systems of regulations and governance. According to Ronald Robertson,

"The expansion of the world religions of Islam and Christianity had an important role in the globalization process. Religion became one of the bases for social transformation both at the level of people's everyday lives and at the national level. If religion was seen as one of the most fundamental means of organizing human life, then the seeds of globalization could be found in religion itself.[1]"

In the village level, Globalization has made its entry into the tribal society through the market and world religion in NE particularly in the hill tribal villages of Manipur. When we trace further more the origin of globalization in the hill tribal society, market system comes at the first even if it is very recent phenomenon. Similar studies were also done by many scholars in the past (see, e.g. Jain 2001; Nayar 2006; Doshi and Jain 1999; Jogdand and Michael 2003 (eds.) *et al.*). On the more important side, the advent of Christianity is the beginning of new globalization in the tribal society in NE particularly in Maram Khullen. So, for tracing the origin of globalization in the tribal society in NE particularly in the hill villages of Manipur, we have to look into two dimensions, namely (1) The formation of market economy in the tribal area/villages, (2) the advent of Christianity in the tribal society.

Market and Tribal Society

Economists have long observed that countries and regions that are linked by common institutions, currencies, or policies, and that enjoy relatively free access to each other's markets, tends to converge to similar levels of income over time (IMF 2006). The earliest form of globalization has been the institution of weekly markets among the tribal. All over the country there has been weekly market in one form or the other among the tribal. These weekly markets were beyond the single village but within a cluster of villages (see, Jain 2001). To understand the globalization in the context of Indian tribal, we must conceptualize the primary units of market economy i.e. weekly market, having a record of about 100 years. And therefore, what we call globalization today is only a recast of weekly markets found among the tribal (Jain 2001 : 3-28).

Globalization has made its entry into the tribal society through the market. Even if the market system is very new in tribal society in NE, its role through which the society enters into globalization is very much remarkable. Before the advent of this present market system, they maintained subsistence economy. They produced their own essential commodities including food and clothing according to their need without hired labour. Commodities were produced from the resources available with them in the village. If there is any surplus over self-consumption, it is bartered or presented to their near and dear one in the village. People of Maram Khullen were making their own cloth from the white cotton planted in the village sufficiently without depending on market and till today some of them in the village are having that hand woven cloth but in a very crude manner. As economy evolves, exceptional needs apart from their own produces in the village were purchased from the nearest market.[2] It is the beginning of socialization and this very socialization changes consumption pattern of the people. It is nothing but the beginning of globalization in any 'other' society in this globe.

Table 5.1 : Modern facilities available in the Village

Item	*Name*	*Distance from the Village (in km)*
Market Place	Maram Centre	4
College	Don Bosco	4
School	John Paul II	0
Post Office	Maram Bazaar	6
Health Centre	Maram Bazaar	6
Tel. Exchange	Maram Bazaar	6
National Highway	NH 39	4

Source : Survey.

Christianity and Maram Khullen

The advent of Christianity in tribal villages in NE is one of the most important factors for entering real globalization into their society. It is not an exaggerating to say that the advent of Christianity is the beginning of globalization in the tribal society in NE. Christianity gives indigenous tribal people new hope and aspiration educationally and spiritually. We have to thank Christianity and western missionary institutions for imparting English education (which is the most important education system in the modern competitive world) to the tribal people. In the words of B. M. Pugh[3], 'the Tribes of NE India today feel greatly indebted to the missionaries of the west for their work of uplifting them'. Origin of the Christianity is concerned in Manipur and Maram Khullen in particular, Rev. William Pettigrew, an Englishman was born in Edinburgh, Scotland arrived at Imphal 1st time on 6th January, 1894 for preaching Christianity. On the 5th March, 1956 Fr. Ravalio and Peter Bianchi, Roman Catholic priests landed up at Imphal. From 1961, Fr. Bianchi started Don Bosco missionary work at Mao-Maram area.[4] Before the advent of Christianity in the Maram Khullen, they were following traditional religion/paganism. But still some of them are following the Paganism in the village (very negligible). They were studying in Manipuri medium with Bengali script, which has limited opportunity in the country. According to the present local *Catechist* (local religious leader of Roman Catholic) of Maram Khullen, N. Kangba Raphael and Karaiba James, lecturer in Political Science (St. Joseph's College, Nagaland), Christian church in the village founded only in 1956.[5] This is the beginning of globalization. Despite one of the biggest tribal villages in Manipur and having around 432 households, there is no proper government educational institution except one Junior High School, which is also not functioning at all. This phenomenon is more or less same in other hill tribal villages in NE region also.

New Wave of Globalization

The earlier integration of the world economy was driven more by technological developments in transportation and communications than by policy changes. But today's most drastic change is in the degree to which government have intervened to reduce obstacles to the flow of trade and investments worldwide. And the new information technologies have created a landscape where movements of services and capital are faster by several orders of magnitudes (Bhagwati 2006 : 11-12). Globalization is not new; recast the early 16th century and the late 19th century. But this era is different from the earlier one. Globalization has been a boon to electronic communication apart from computer and software. Recently in 2005, Maram Khullen has got the facilities of Mobile network, Internet, DTH television/radio channel. It is nothing but a new wave of globalization in this region.

The new wave of globalization is the globalization by *Air not by road like before* (Mathew and Singha 2006). This new wave of globalization is very much different from the earlier type of globalization especially in the tribal society in NE. Old system of globalization could not reach tribal hinterland but this new wave of globalization reaches every nook and corner of this globe because it is the globalization by air, not by road. There is no landline telephone connection in this village till today but after the advent of this new wave of globalization, they can get mobile network properly even if government cannot install exchange centre in the village. And so far the internet facility is concerned, this village can avail 24-hours internet facility from the Don Bosco College, which is hardly 4 km from the village.

Impact of Globalization

To begin with, globalization itself is a social phenomenon of systematic proportions, embodying contradictory processes and different cross-currents. Fukuyama (1992) opines that globalization is the only institution in the world which unites the human society, and the rest will be disappearing gradually. Again, no single variable can explain such a broad and multi-faceted phenomenon as the economy. So, the impact of globalization has become a debatable issue among the intellectuals and policy-makers. There is a big block of anti-globalization movement in the developing nations which sees only pessimistic side of the globalization. And on the other block of the advanced nations, is optimistic side of the globalization looking for big market and global competition. It is still inconclusive and has got mixed response in India.

When this globalization comes to a village level, a question that arises; what will happen to a tribal village economy/society if it reaches to the grassroot level? This is the core issue of this chapter and tries to draw a conclusion by analyzing Maram Khullen village. Globalization, when it comes down to a village level particularly in Maram Khullen, its situation becomes different from the global phenomenon. Whatsoever, the reason, the impact of globalization is to be discussed in two different ways: (1) Negative aspects, and (2) Positive aspects in Maram Khullen.

Negative Aspects of Globalization

The Dean of Marxist economists in India, Prabhat Patnaik offers an exemplary articulation of the contra position. In a wide-ranging attack in which he uses the term "*globalization and imperialism*" alternatively to describe the same phenomenon and he claims that :

> *The net result, taking the Third World as a whole, of surrendering to the process of globalization in this sense is : relative economic stagnation, increased income*

> *inequalities leading to a worsening of poverty, a loss of economic and political sovereignty ... a loss of control over domestic assets and natural resources to metropolitan capital, and the loss of food security.*[6]

With the advent of new wave of globalization, the sense of vulnerability or economic security, is arguably greater today than in earlier periods because the growing integration of nations worldwide into the international economy, has intensified competitive pressures from actual and potential rival elsewhere. It is also easily seen that indigenous people have suffered grossly at the hand of bigger and advanced groups. The biggest worry seems to have been that they would lose their lands because the governments of the countries in which the indigenous groups were supplanted by intruding colonialists and settlers in the last two centuries appear to have turned to legal doctrines such as the theory of *terra nullius* (under which communal rights to "unoccupied" land are not recognized). Such doctrines have made it easier to deprive the indigenous groups of their traditional right to deny legal purchase by others of such lands (Bhagwati 2006 : 114).

In the same manner, Jain (2001) has rightly observed that globalization has also proved to be destructive in some aspect of culture. The western culture tends to dominate over the indigenous culture. It produces a downward pressure for local autonomy and regional reforms. Local culture would always be at the verge of extinction. Not only the culture but the local economy would always be disturbed. For instance, the locally made artefacts and handicrafts would decay at the onslaught of the products made from the outside. This will discourage the initiative and creativity of the indigenous people in the tribal villages. As a result of which handloom and handicraft goods of tribal people in Manipur became a show piece in the museum.

Economy evolves in the tune of social and cultural

structure in the society. As the social structure changes, the consumption pattern and the direction of the economy also changes in the direction. With the advent of modern wave of globalization, the basic structure of Maram Khullen village has been displaced. Folk culture, songs and traditional music are replaced by the rock and pop music of west. They are attracted by the fashionable dresses, bourgeois life-style and consumption habit of west shown by the television and other electronic media. They have all drown in the conspicuous consumption which leads them to impoverish. There is a wide gap between income and expenditure flow in the tribal economy. It is perhaps due to the westernization (not modernization) influenced by the electronic media, television, cinema and modern globalization.[7] Domestic producing units and cottage industries are compelled to shut down as the economy turns away towards the west. So far as the co-operation and helping hand is concerned in Maram Khullen, traditionally, the construction of a dwelling house, hands of the whole village were extended. If anybody fails to help, he feels guilty but it seems to be disappeared now from this village.

Individualism and materialism became very prominent in the village. Consumption of daily life in the village from down to dusk is the products of Multi National Corporations (MNCs) from outside. As Balance of Payment of the poor countries deteriorates when they trade with developed countries, village economy suffers when it is opened to the global markets. With the influence of new globalization wave, people of this village have accustomed to fashionable dresses, hair fixer, lipstick, perfume, face cream, tobacco and foreign liquor, etc. Before the arrival of new wave of globalization, people of this village were weaving their own cloth but now-a-days no one is weaving the cloth.

Positive Aspects of Globalization

India has doubtless made considerable accommodation to

globalization since the last decade of the 20th century, if not earlier. Contrary to the position of the critics of globalization, who emphasize economic stagnation as its likely outcome, the empirical data on economic growth rates leave no doubt that the opening to globalization has been enormously beneficial for economic growth in India. Rather than the economic stagnation, globalization has led to the acceleration of the growth rate on literally every count; criticism of globalization seems groundless.[8] In a market economy, employment and wages have been largely influenced by the integration of the labour supply and demand, rather than by government legislation or union pressure. Such flexible markets have encouraged efficient allocation of workers across sectors, higher investment and use of more labour intensive technologies. This has resulted in more rapid output growth, which in turn has enhanced labour demand, employment and wages. The cycle has been reinforced by the high levels of education, vocational training and health care that have allowed the pattern of employment more skilled-intensive, again supporting rising wages and living standards.[9]

Globalization has been a boon to electronic communication apart from computer and software. Recently since 2005, Maram Khullen village has got mobile network, internet, DTH (Direct to Home) Radio/TV channel. Before that, the village could not receive any sort of TV and Radio channel properly. Now with DTH dish antenna costing hardly Rs. 2000, they can get world's information in this remote village. They can enjoy News Headline, DD news, Ajtak and Gyan Darshan freely. Is not it advanced of electronic technology? Despite being a biggest and oldest village among the Marams, government has not provided land line telephone connection till date. Since it is one of the villages on the high hill top, they can get mobile network easily from different exchanges. Road connecting to village from the NH 39 which is hardly 4 km has been made motorable in 2004 only. Now there is regular passenger Sumo and mini bus service from village. And so far quality education is concerned; this village has got best college in Manipur[10] offering all the three streams with internet service. Thanks to the Christian Missionary Institution (Catholic Mission) for imparting quality and English education in this village.

Findings of Globalization in the Village

In the era of 21st century, there is no real alternative to globalization. If countries want to develop economically, they have to participate actively in the international exchange of goods, services, technology, money and people.[11] As stated above, it is the *globalization by air not by road*. Whether we like it or not, we cannot escape from this new wave of globalization. No agent can resist or impose this new wave of globalization. It is an automatic and spontaneous process in the global development movement. We cannot say that no TV network, internet and mobile signal should come to their territory. And on the other hand, it is the most essential infrastructure for long-term development of a society. No doubt, it has some inconveniences in the beginning but that will be automatically adjusted by the global market mechanism/globalization process. One thing is true in this village that the most important investment of long-term development like, education and basic infrastructure is moving to a right direction. Once the basic infrastructures are put, growth/development in the village is spontaneous. This is what we need in the tribal society or any other remote villages.

Since this new wave of globalization is inevitable, it is better to harness it before it is too late. We should not delay, let us embrace it and make use of it in right manner. Despite having some negative points, globalization brought this village (Maram Khullen) into a new height, especially in the field of education. If this sector develops, the rest will be taken care of by it and this village will develop further very shortly.

Some Suggestions

In the popular phrasing of the politicians who join the anti-globalization group that, globalization needs a human face. Yet, this does not mean that globalization left to itself, will produce the best, as distinct from generally good results. Bhagwati (2006) "If what I have written so far has been read with care, it should be clear that, in many ways globalization will yield better results if it is managed."

Globalization should not be thought of as a solution to everything. It merely provides opportunities. Those who take advantage, they flourish and those who do not they sink. Globalization is not supposed to produce equality of outcome but it produces equality of opportunity for those with right mindset. Hence, the developing countries/poor village economies have to focus on economic restructuring, building market supporting institutions and creating efficient regulatory mechanisms. Globalization should not be accused for loosing share of the low income countries/poor village economy. These countries suffer from internal problems like rapid rise in population, infrastructure bottlenecks, and weak financial markets and so on. More access to globalization and its benefits demand that developing countries/poor economies first put in place a necessary conducive environment to ensure higher returns and larger markets for foreign investors.

To get a share of global capital, technology and output, village economies/developing countries have to upgrade their social and economic institutions through administrative, legislative and legal reforms.[12] New wave of globalization is a sort of re-incarnation for Maram Khullen. And this phenomenon is more or less same to all the tribal villages in NE. We can develop the traditional artefacts, hand loom and handicrafts in the tune to new system. With the notion of *think globally and act locally*, we should not be drowning ourselves into the other's lifestyle. Very often, we are attracted by the lifestyle of west shown in the cinema and TV. Development process in the village can be guided by the knowledge. In this context, M.K. Gandhi has rightly said :[13]

> *I do not want my house to be walled in on all sides and windows stuffed. I want the cultures of all the lands to be blown about my house as freely as possible. But I refuse to be blown of my feet. I refuse to live in other's houses as an interloper, a beggar or a slave.*

NOTES & REFERENCES

1. See Leela D'Souza's paper "Globalization and Religious Fundamentalist Movements : A search for identity" in P.G. Jogdand and S.M.Michael (2003 Eds.) "*Globalization and Social Movements : Struggle for Humane Society*", Rawat Publications, Jaipur, pp. 55 - 63.
2. Maram Khullen people used to go down to Maram Bazar on the NH 39 or Senapati district headquarters and even to Imphal).
3. As quoted by Jeyaseelan (1996) "*Impact of the Missionary Movement in Manipur*", Scholar Publishing House Pvt. Ltd., New Delhi.
4. *Ibid.* p, 74.
5. That is why they are celebrating golden jubilee of the village catholic church in December 2006 in commemoration of the foundation of the church in the village.
6. See Baldev Raj Nayar (2006) : "India's Globalization : Evaluating the Economic Consequences", East-west Center, Washington DC, pp. 2-3.

7. Singha, Komol (2005) : "Demonstration Effect in Economic Development in Tribal Economy" on 21st April 2005 in local daily *"The Sangai Express"*, Imphal.
8. See, Nayar 2006:2-79
9. G. Raju (2001) : "How the liberalization works for the rural poor", *Southern Economists,* Sept. 1, 2001, Bangalore.
10. One of the best colleges in Manipur , Don Bosco College is just below the Maram Khullen foothill
11. S. Rangachar former staff member of the World Bank, Washington D C, USA.
12. M. Mallick and J. Lenka (2006). "Globalization and Development : Disaggregate Dynamics", *Southern Economist,* 15 Jan 2006, Bangalore.
13. Tomlinson, J. (1999) : *Globalisation and Culture.* Chicago : Chicago University Press.

6

Income and Consumption Pattern

In the previous chapters we have dealt with different sectors which influence the development and formation of a village economy. This chapter deals with income and expenditure pattern (only accounting/visible income and expenditure) of a tribal village in their development trajectory. A glimpse of income patterns and consumption which help in determining economic status of the village is studied. For convenience of the study, this chapter is classified into five occupational categories of the people/household in the village. Those are as follows : (1) Salaried group (Govt.); (2) Salaried group (Private); (3) Business or Self-enterprise; (4) Cultivator; and (5) Other category which includes jobless, retired people, casual workers.

Like any other tribal villages, Maram Khullen is also a predominantly agricultural village. They live mainly on the subsistence income from the agriculture, forest produces and partially from the government job. Due to the scarcity of resources, some of families have taken up self-employment activities but the number of businessmen is very negligible. Like any other rural communities in the country, government job is the primary target of this village and others follow.

The survey result (Table 6.1) reveals that family lives on government salary occupy 19 per cent (81 families) in the

Table 6.1 : Occupational Structure in the Village

Occupational Category	*No. of Households*	*No. of people live on (as main occupation)*
Employee (Govt.)	81 (19)	141 (6)
Employee (Private)	17 (4)	90 (4)
Business/Self-employed	39 (9)	64 (3)
Cultivator	282 (65)	736 (31)
Others including retired	13 (3)	1331* (56)
Total	**432** (100)	**2376** (100)

Source : Survey.

Note. Figures in the parenthesis refer to percentage of the total number.

*1. It includes Jobless, Children and Old age people and Retired.

village, and 141 persons i.e. 6 per cent of the total population in the village are government employees. The second category occupation is the employees in the private farms which consists of 4 per cent (17 households) of the total households in the village and in terms of total number of people working in private firm is also 4 per cent (90 people in the village). It is followed by business or self-employed households, which occupies 9 per cent (39 families) of the total households in the village and in terms of people engaged in the field are 64 people (3 per cent of the total population in the village). Cultivation occupies the highest percentage of the family i.e. 65 per cent of the total households (282 families) in the village. Similarly, number of people willingly or unwillingly engaged in cultivation as main occupation is 736 (31 per cent). The remaining families or people are clubbed together as other category.

Table 6.2 : Category-wise Household Average Annual Income-Expenditure Pattern

Household Occupational Category	*Household Average Annual Income in Rs.*	*Household Average Annual Expenditure in Rs.*	*Differences*
Employee (Govt.)	1,46,333	1,43,549	+2,784
Employee (Private)	1,58,400	2,52,825	-9,44,425
Business/Self-enterprise	1,28,000	2,07,558	-79,558
Cultivator	5,9,284	96,212	-36,928

Source : Survey.

Source of Income

Table 6.3 highlights the income contributed by different sectors in the village economy. The highest contribution to the total income of the village (calculated from the 202 sampled households) is made by the agricultural sector amounting to Rs. 219 lakhs annually. It occupies a share of approximately 59 per cent to the total income in the village. Salary sector occupies second position in contributing village economy amounting to Rs. 61 lakhs, whose share to the total village income is approximately 16.48 per cent. The contribution of business or self-enterprise in the village economy is not that much significant, amounting to approximately Rs. 4 lakhs and occupies 1.08 per cent to the total income of the village annually. Despite being closely connected with forest and hill, the contribution of horticulture and forest to the village income is very meagre. They constitute 0.12 per cent and 0.22 per cent respectively (total to Re. 0.48 and Re. 0.81 lakhs respectively) to the village income.

Table 6.3 : Village income from different sources (amount in terms of lakhs)

Source	*Per cent*	*Total*
Agriculture	59.1	219.44
Salaried	16.48	61.21
Business	1.08	4.32
Horticulture	0.12	0.48
Forest and Handloom	0.22	0.81
Others*	23	85.79
Total	100	371

Source : Survey.

* Others include broadly grant and gift, poultry and piggery, hunting, casual worker and animal husbandry etc.

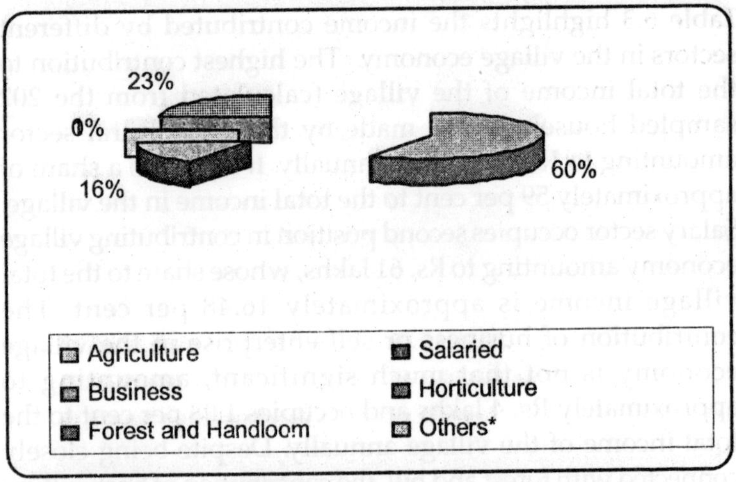

Fig. 6.1 : Percentage of income under different sources.

* Others include broadly grant and gift, poultry and piggery, hunting, casual worker and animal husbandry, etc.

Table 6.2 reveals the rough idea of income and expenditure balance sheet of the village economy. The government employee household category (19 per cent of the total households constitutes the employee household category in the village) has got positive annual income. The average annual income is Rs. 1,46,333 and average annual expenditure is Rs. 1,43,549, and the balance is positive i.e. +Rs. 2,784. Whereas, remaining occupational household categories have gone to negative balance of annual income. The average annual income of employee in private farm household category is Rs. 1,58,000 and the average annual household expenditure is Rs. 2,52,825, and the balance between two is negative (Rs. -9,44,425). Similarly, business self-employed household category is also going to negative income balance. Though the percentage of this category is very small (9 per cent or 39 families in the village), the annual average income is only Rs. 1,28,000 and the corresponding annual average expenditure of this category is Rs. 2,07,558. So, the balance between the two is also negative; i.e. Rs. -79,558. Finally, the cultivation household category which constitutes largest number in the village (65 per cent to the total households in the village) is also gone to negative average annual income. The annual average income of this category is Rs. 59,284 and average annual household expenditure is Rs. 96,212 and the balance between two goes to pretty negative; i.e. Rs. -36,928 annually.

Items of Consumption

Individual items of expenditure may now be taken up to have a synoptic view of the consumption pattern in the village as a whole. Survey reveals that the village spends approximately Rs. 511 lakhs and earns hardly Rs. 371 lakhs monthly. This clearly shows that the expenditure is greater than the income in the village economy. How do they manage? This argument will be dealt at the end of this chapter.

Table 6.4 : Expenditure structure of the Village (amount in terms of lakhs)

Item	*Per cent*	*Total*
Food	37.11	190
Stationery	18.16	93
Consumer Durable	22.92	117
Education	16.06	82
Medical	1.61	8
Intoxicant	4.11	21
Total	100	511

Source : Survey.

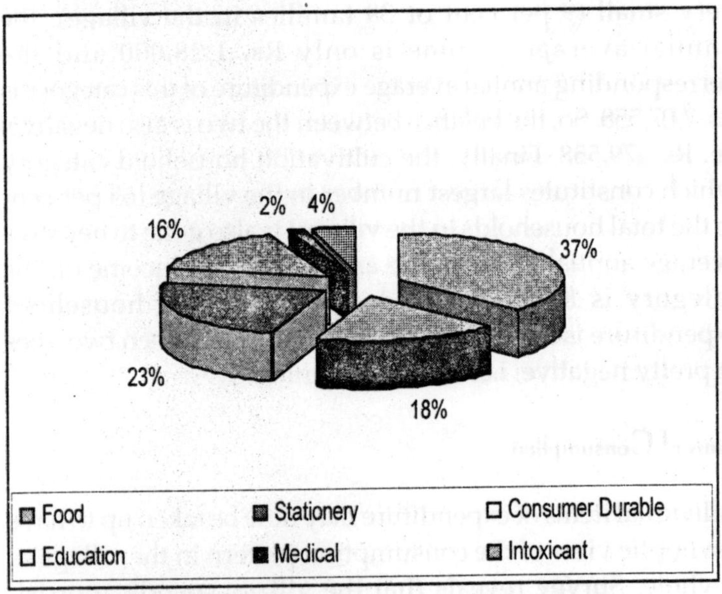

Fig. 6.2 : Share of expenditure on different items

The expenditure on food occupies highest percentage in the village income expenditure data sheet (Table 6.4). The approximate expenditure on food items is Rs. 190 lakhs which constitutes 37.11 per cent of the total expenditure in the village. It is followed by consumer durable items which constitute around 23 per cent or roughly Rs. 117 lakhs. The next significant items are Non-durable consumer goods (Stationery items) and expenditure on education. They constitute 18.16 and 16.06 per cent respectively of the total expenditure in the village economy. They are roughly Rs. 93 lakhs and Rs. 82 lakhs respectively.

Interestingly, the expenditure on education (16.06 per cent) of this village compared to other villages in the national level is quite impressive and it helps in faster development of the village. On the contrary, the expenditure on health is too small and expenditure on intoxicant items is quite high. The expenditure on health and medicine is hardly 1.61 per cent of the total expenditure; it is roughly Rs. 8 lakhs. The expenditure on intoxicant items is approximately Rs. 21 lakhs, and occupies a share of 4.11 per cent to the total expenditure.

Expenditure on Food Items

The percentage of overall expenditure on food items in the village is 37.11 out of the total village expenditure spent on (Table 6.4). The four groups of families in the village are spending from about 24 to 41 per cent of their total expenditure on food items (Table 6.5). The expenditure of cultivation class (65 per cent of households in the village) registered highest percentage of their expenditure on food items, roughly about Rs.112.5 lakhs (40.81 per cent). Business or self-enterprise family too shares slightly lower than the former class. Though number of family of this category is very small (9 per cent), the percentage of expenditure on food item is 40.29 which is approximately a total amount of Rs. 5 lakhs. The employee (government) class follows third in the hierarchal list of consumption on food items in the village. This class spends 33 per cent of their total expenditure on food items that is Rs. 38,19,858. Families living on salaries from private firm spend least percentage on food items i.e. 23.86 per cent of their total expenditure (Rs. 3,01,680).

Expenditure on Education

The most interesting part in the study of expenditure pattern of this village is the expenditure on education. The average percentage of expenditũre spends on education by all sections of the household in the village is 16.06 per cent of the total expenditure in the village (Table 6.4). Though this village is the lone primitive tribe in the State, the expenditure on education is quite high and impressive. The category belongs to government employee which constitutes 19 per cent (81 families) of the total household in the village spends 22 per cent of their total expenditure on education (Table 6.5). Unlike other farmer category in the national level, this village's cultivation class constituting 65 per cent of the total household in the village spend 17.10 per cent of their total expenditure. The third significant category is business/self-enterprise (9 per cent of the total households in the village); whose percentage of expenditure on education is 9.26 per cent. Unfortunately, the family category belongs to employee in the private firm spend much lesser than the other occupational categories in the village. They hardly spend 5 per cent (Rs. 58,560) of their total expenditure on education.

Expenditure on Consumer Goods (Non-durable)

The expenditure on stationery items in the village is 18.16 per cent (Table 6.4). In case of class-wise consumption on stationery item; employee class in the private firm spends a total of 29.82 per cent of their total expenditure (Table 6.5). It is followed by business class households. They spend 20.13 per cent constituting a total amount of Rs. 2,50,320 of their expenditure on this item.

Table 6.5 : Category-wise Expenditure Pattern in the Village

(*amount in Rs.*)

Commodity/ Item	*Cultivator*	*Business/Self-enterprise*	*Employee (Private)*	*Employee (Govt.)*
Food	1,12,58,208 (40.81)	5,00,832 (40.29)	3,01,680 (23.86)	38,19,858 (33)
Stationery	43,72,800 (15.85)	2,50,320 (20.13)	3,77,088 (29.82)	20,24,420 (17)
Consumer Durable	55,13,856 (19.98)	3,33,600 (26.84)	4,75,920 (37.64)	24,85,864 (21)
Education	47,17,296 (17.10)	1,15,200 (9.26)	58,560 (4.63)	26,09,053 (22)
Health	6,06,144 (2.19)	3,840 (0.30)	3,360 (0.26)	1,54,701 (1.4)
Intoxicant	11,17,632 (4.05)	39,120 (3.14)	47,520 (3.75)	6,05,709 (5)
Total	**2,75,85,936 (100)**	**12,42,912 (100)**	**12,64,128 (100)**	**1,16,99,605 (100)**

Source : Survey.

Note: Figures in the parenthesis are the percentage of the total.

The government employee section spends comparatively less percentage of their income on stationery items. They spend hardly 17 per cent (Rs. 20,24,420) of their total expenditure on stationery items in the village. And, finally farmer class in the village spends 15.86 per cent of their total expenditure on stationery items. It constitutes approximately an amount of Rs. 43,72,800 of the village income.

Expenditure on Consumer Durables

Consumption on consumer durables is one of the important indicators of economic status in an economy. Very interestingly, employee in the private firm category in the village spends highest percentage of their expenditure on consumer durable items i.e. 37.64 per cent and the rough total amount is Rs. 4,75,920. It is followed by the business class or self-enterprise category with 26.84 per cent of the total amount of expenditure (Table 6.5). The third significant category is the government employee class. Despite they have handsome annual income; they spend a total amount of Rs. 24,85,864 on consumer durable items (21 per cent of total expenditure) in the village. The cultivator class spends 19.98 per cent of their total expenditure on consumer durable items. It comes to the approximately a total amount of Rs. 55,13,856 of the total village expenditure.

Expenditure on Health

The average expenditure on health and medicine in the village is quite low compared to other items (Table 6.5). Though the share of consumption on health sector in the village is very low, the farmer category spends the highest percentage on medicine/health. They spend 2.19 per cent of their total expenditure on health/medicine; which constitutes an amount of Rs. 6,06,144. It is followed by government employee section; they spend 1.4 per cent of their total expenditure (Rs. 1,54,701). The business class and the employee in private firm spend 0.30 and 0.26 per cent respectively. This shows that the poor farmer section of the people in the village spends more percentage of their expenditure on medicine and the employee in the private firm class spends least percentage of expenditure on medicine.

Expenditure on Intoxicants

Table 6.5 shows that the percentage of expenditure spent on intoxicants is quite higher than other villages in the national level. The employee class consumes comparatively more than other classes of the households in the village. This category of households spends 5 per cent of their total expenditure on intoxicant items. It constitutes a total amount of Rs. 6,05,709 out of the total expenditure Rs. 1,16,99,605. The cultivator class spends 4.05 per cent (Rs. 11, 17,632) of their total expenditure on intoxicants like liquor, tobacco and Zarda, etc. It is followed very closely by business and private employee class with 3.14 and 3.75 per cent respectively.

Analysis of the Data

We have learnt from the above facts that the income and expenditure pattern of this village is confined to the four major occupational categories falling within our sample survey. The income and expenditure balance data sheet shows negative income except government employee class. It is not so in reality; the gap is filled up by non-market economy or unrecorded factors. They normally calculate only the monetary transaction in the village economy, ignoring the non-monetary sectors. This is the reason why government employee class has got positive income balance. Secondly, majority of the household in the village cannot give exact monetary account because the village economy involves partly non-monetary sector or informal economy. There is partly non-existence of market and subsistence economy system in this village still. But the main purpose of consumption pattern analysis was served with this sample data.

The more interesting part in this chapter is the higher percentage of expenditure on education. Approximately 17 percentage of expenditure on education in a hill tribal village is quite impressive. It is hardly 6 to 9 per cent in other backward villages in the national level and the government employee category spends 22 per cent of their total expenditure on education which is much higher than the national level. A society can develop at the very fast rate if percentage of expenditure to the total expenditure of the society is approximately 20 per cent (See, Tilak 2005). It is also clear that this village could change in the developmental front rapidly in this decade because they embrace English education.

In the part of the consumption of intoxicants, the percentage of intoxicant consumption in this village is 4.11 per cent of their income. The relationship between the consumption of intoxicant and development of the society is negative. Consumption of intoxicant increases and leads health hazards in the society and consequently in the economy. Being a primitive tribe, the level of consumption of intoxicant is not so big and most of them are brewing at home.

The percentage of consumption on medicine or health is much lower (1.61 per cent) than other villages particularly in the valley. Basically, the relationship between health and economy is somewhat positive. In the case of this village, they spend less percentage on health/medicine because they rely on traditional healing system and herbal medicine available in the village. Secondly, chemist shop and medical facility is also not available in the village. Thirdly, since they are the hill dweller and movement/exercise of body is much more than the people in the valley, so the immune system for protecting from minor disease is very strong.

One more peculiar characteristic of the hill people is the consumption of consumer goods and consumer durables. They do not have much interest in buying costly golden jewellery items. The habit of accumulating durable goods is less and they are basically hedonistic in nature. Banking habit and investment in the productive activities are ignorant of this people.

7

Social, Physical and Human Capital

In the previous chapter consumption pattern was discussed as an integral part in forming village economy. To evaluate more detail of the village structure especially in the hill village, this chapter examines three important capitals which are very much important for economic development. For rural development to succeed in a global environment, three things are essential : Human Capital, Physical Infrastructure, and adequate financing. We agree that human capital and physical infrastructure (Public capital) are critical components of sustainable community development. However, we feel that the third element should be social capital. Communities that have thriving social networks and institutions and good human capital will have adequate financing as well (Rainey, *et al.* 2003). It is nothing but the Public capital, Human capital, and Social capital are the three forms of capital that are the essential for sustainable community development. Communities , who want to participate in the global economy must be able to provide access to quality communication and transportation infrastructure and outstanding amenities. All these three capitals are discussed one by one in detail below :

Social Capital

The social capital, as Putnam (1993) defines the norms, networks, and social trust that make society/community function more smoothly. Granovetter (1985) finds that the social capital theory explains development from a structural rather than an economic perspective. Its emphasis is on the 'embeddedness' within which economic relations take place, based on the notion that both individual and group decisions are embedded in a particular social context that includes community traditions, norms, networks, and the like. Basu (2008) also incorporated the idea of 'social norms' in functioning trade or economic system smoothly in a society. The social capital theory is situated in a growing body of literature that seeks to challenge the idea that only the market-driven path of development can lead to improved social and economic conditions (Rainey 2003:708-15). The diversity of village institutions is instrumental in how government policies and economy, and environmental changes affect village economic activities and incomes (Taylor and Adelman 1996:14-15). In the first phase, the village community is primarily a political society, in the second a body of co-owners of the soil, while in the third phase it becomes the emblem of traditional economy and polity (Dumont 1957). So, the community (village community for this purpose) bounded by a well-articulated norms is the prerequisite for sustainable economic development in the globalized world.

Community literally means a group of people stand together for common interest or common cause. A traditional view on 'community' in sociology, from Karl Marx to Ferdinand Tonnies and Max Weber, has been to assume a small group of people (or families) bounded by blood and locational ties, in which different economic principles operate from those of the capitalist economy is primitive profit-seeking by individuals. The principle of community is mutual help for guaranteeing subsistence to all its members. In the past, traditional communities such as tribes and villages have been regarded as a yoke or fetter on modernization. Theoretically, communities range from family to the national community and further to the 'global' or 'international' community (Hayami and Godo 2006:310-28). However, the community discussed in this chapter covers only a village level community (Maram Khullen).

Table 7.1 : Moieties-Clans/Sub-clans in the Village

Section/Colony/Sagei	*Moiety*	*Clan*
Makha Sagei	Ng'kiikui/	1. Kishumai
	Kagamna	2. Majangmai
		3. Puinamai
Khullakpa Sagei	Dikakuina/	1. Dinamei
	Lamkhana	2. Rangnamei
		3. Karangnamei
Mathak Sagei	RangbiingRaiyinamai/	1. Magai-Bognamai
	Magai-Bognamai	2. Bishunggnamai

Source : Compiled from Athickal (1992: 54) and James Karaiba's report.

Note : These clans have many sub-clans and these sub-clans take after the name of the one from whom it is descended.

The Maram society is a patrilineal society. The principle of primogeniture is strictly followed. The eldest surviving son succeeds to a clan headmanship. The *Sagong*[1] is the de facto and dejure head of village; he is the executive, legislative and judicial authority. The present day welfare schemes and governmental projects are handled through the office of the *Khullakpa*[2] (Athickal 1992:61-63). According to James Karaiba an educationist of the village, in hierarchical order, each *Sagei*[3] (Makha, Khullakpa and Mathak) is headed by a Chairman, and *Sagong* is the over all chief (King of the village) of the three *Sageis* in the village.

Any matter related to a Sagei is discussed and resolved within the Sagei. If the issue is not resolved within the Sagei, it will be brought out by their respective Chairman in the Village Council. Profit motive organization is concerned in the village, there is a Women Self-Help Group (SHG), called 'Women SHG, Maram Khullen' consisting of 12 sub-groups under the aegis of IFAD. Commercial farming like Potato, Passion fruit and Tree-tomato cultivation were their main activities. Whatever, the profit generated from farming was pooled together to the mother association (Women SHG, Maram Khullen) and bought a vehicle (Tata Sumo) for commercial purposes. The same vehicle is still plying as local taxi from Maram Khullen to Senapati, district headquarter. Unfortunately, with the fall of the activities of IFAD in the village, all the farming activities of the 12 sub-groups have become dormant.

Table 7.2 : Organizations in the Village and their Activities

Name	*Nature*	*Activity*	*Cover Area*	*Approx. Members*
Maram Khullen Village Council	Non-Profit Organization	Socio-economic and political activity	Entire Village	Min. 4 members from each Sagei + Sagong
Maram Khullen Youth Club	Non-Profit Organization	Developmental Activities	Entire Village	All Young People in the village
Maram Khullen Students' Union	Non-Profit Organization	Educational and Developmental	All students in the village	All students in the village
Women SHGs Maram Khullen	Profit-motive •	Agriculture/ Farming	4 SHGs in each Sagei	20-25 members

Source : Survey

Note : Some names of the SHGs are Apailabapui, Rairai-namei, Bisii-namei, Bisung-namei, Huibi-namei, etc.

Development of a village whether it is hill or valley, the role of the society which the village owns is very important.

In the process of planning, implementation, monitoring, evaluation and benefit sharing system, etc., community's or people's active participation is required. It is found in the past studies of the scholars like (Ao 1993; Debnath 2007; Singha 2007 etc.). Because much of the success of the Maram Khullen entirely depends on how the community or the people take initiative directly or indirectly in the village. Hayami and Godo (2006) argue that the community is the organization that guides community members to voluntary cooperation based upon close personal ties and mutual trust.

Research by Rainey *et al.* (2003) and others suggest though economics can say a lot about the efficiency impacts from the changes in the distribution on income, the proper distribution should be determined by society through market operations or government intervention if society deems that the markets are doing a poor job. Social capital or village community, in the form of trust, reduces transaction costs and increases accountability on a more local level. It has been shown to increase the economic opportunities of the poor and to give the disenfranchised increased participation in government. The law of tribal village institution is so strong and powerful that there is no such case which the village council cannot settle within the village. The situation is same in Maram Khullen also. Members in the village community are strongly locked in to the social norm of the village or community. Social and community function cannot be avoided in the village. Any body who ignores it will be fined heavily by the village community. No individual can violate village and customary law. Village Council headed by *Sagong* has got full judiciary power in the village and no State interference is needed. This is the reason why the role of State judiciary court procedures is not noticed in the tribal villages. Moreover, where Judges and police are not necessarily the faithful agents of citizens, it can happen that the market failures are not only not corrected but even enlarged by government failures. Third-party mediation, especially formal court procedure, entails significant costs and thus it does not pay to apply it to conflicts involving small sums of money (Hayami and Godo, 2006 : 314). There is no threat on individual property by any thief or burglar in the village. If there is any, he/she can be napped and justice is done very easily within the village itself. Unlike government court, village law is very much impartial and very fast in delivering justice.

Trust is the social capital, which can reduce social transaction cost (see, e.g. Hayami and Godo 2006; Putnam 1993). In Maram Khullen, the role of village council or student organization is very great, and community members are strongly locked in with the trust and the beliefs of the village social system. Trust accumulated through the personal interactions in the community increases efficiency and reduces costs associated with the division of labour as done in the classical economics. In this regard, trust is a kind of 'social capital' similar to social overhead capital such as roads and harbours (Arrow 1974; Dasgupta 1988; Putnam 1993; Seabright 1993). Helping hand and benevolent service to the poor or needy villagers by the well-to-do or rich man in the village is a sort of pride and status on the part of the latter. The *Morung System* is an example of it. Landless people in the village and any body who wants to be a part of their member in the village are provided with a plot of land from the village land or clan land. They have the system of hired-labour within the village particularly during the harvesting season and repay it in the form of labour when needed. Till very recently, when a family cuts/prepares hill slope (waste land) for terrace paddy field, whole villagers join. Construction of a house in the village was supported labour by whole village and anybody misses it feels very guilty. These systems are no more in the village now.

Now the question that arises is how far the model fits to the existing village system. Practically, social and traditional norms of this village have little significance on the new global economic order especially in this transitional stage. Any of the village institutions mentioned above could not save the dying passion fruit farms in Maram Khullen funded by IFAD. Failure of the water supply project during eighties in the village was an example of lacking policy and planning in the village council or community.[4] There are ample of examples in the village in which village institutions fail to protect the public goods, e.g. Public health centre, Government Junior High School are not functioning at all. These village institutions are more concerned with the social and political activities. It may probably be due to deep rooted subsistence system of economy in the village and so to say that basically political and social activities were more important in the village. In the study of Rainey *et al.* (2003) and others also opine that many local economies have stagnated or declined because leaders are too concerned about protecting the special interests of a small group of people. Almost all the employees of non-functioning public institutions are from the well-to-do village leaders' family and they live mainly in the urban areas. They prefer immediate and direct benefit whichever the possible sources. This is evident from the smooth functioning of mid-day meal for students by the Integrated Child Development Services (ICDS) even if school is not functioning. Nobody is there to ask why and how these government institutions got failed. Any external funding projects in the village, especially government, are considered as free goods. Recently[5], Airtel (Mobile Phone) company came to install a tower as a part of expanding their network in the rural areas and since this village is on the top of the hill, it is very much convenient to cover larger network. But unfortunately, at the time of field survey, the said company could not execute their work due to huge ransom demand by the underground. Now the question is where the village authority has gone?

North (1994) refers, "The traditional norms and beliefs deeply rooted in people's minds, are more difficult to change than formal laws so that they are likely to become more fetters on modern economic development." It is termed as "Bonding Capital" by Woolcock (2001). Community institutions and organizations are inflexible and fail to adjust to changing economic needs. Traditional norms and conventions in communities have been formed slowly over many, many years (Hayami and Godo, 2006 : 346). Even after conversion to Christianity, society cannot completely ignore the traditional ritual and social practices.[6] The same result is also found in the study of Hann (1980) and others in the past. So, they cannot easily adjust with the modern changing world.

Physical Infrastructure

Infrastructure is the set of interconnected structural elements that provide the framework for supporting the entire structure and includes a broad spectrum of services, institutions and facilities that ranges from transportation systems and public utilities to finance systems, laws and law enforcement, education and research (Singha and Kabra 2008). It comprises of basic services without which primary, secondary and tertiary productive activities cannot function (Ganapathi and Seethalakshmy 2007). Communities that want to participate in the global economy must be able to provide access to quality communication and transportation infrastructure and outstanding amenities. Communities that are deficient in these areas will find themselves at a considerable disadvantage for attracting and/or maintaining firms in a global environment (Rainey *et al.* 2003). Physical infrastructure covering *transportation, power and communication* through its backward and forward linkages facilitates growth; social infrastructure including water supply, sanitation, sewage disposal, education and health, which are in the nature of primary services, has a direct impact on the quality of life. It is the prerequisite condition for economic development in the world.

Regarding sustainable economic development policies, Harrison says, "I also define 'productive' local economic development policy (as contrasted with a tax- and wage-cutting race to the bottom, in which localities compete with one another by reducing their standard of living) as the building on stronger attractors for catching multi-locational or networked capital. This is done by providing high-quality infrastructure—roads, bridges, waste disposal, telecommunications, transportation and highly skilled labour". Quality infrastructure enhances the quality of life especially in the villages.

Table 7.3 shows some basic physical infrastructure and their present condition. Government (primary) school is almost dead due to their (villagers) negligence. The Head master of this school is from Imphal but he never comes to the school. Whenever, School inspector comes for inspection, he then only comes. It means he has tied up with the village leaders as well as the school inspector. No student is enrolled practically now but for the sake of Mid-day meal, ICDS workers bring some poor villagers and make them attend the meal. It is because ICDS employees need not only salary but also the materials/food items given for the students.

On the other hand, private school run by Christian Missionary 'John Paul II' is functioning smoothly. Villagers are sending their children to private school and ready to pay more tuition fee for the sake of good education. Regarding the higher secondary school and college they have got one of the best colleges (with internet facility) in Manipur. 'Don Bosco College' at Maram Centre is just on the foothill of Maram Khullen. It is also run by Christian Missionary. Post office and Bank are there at Maram Bazaar, it is 5-6 km away on the way from the village. This village is well connected with power supply. Though they cannot get land line telephone, at least they can enjoy BSNL mobile network because of the telephone exchange at Maram Bazaar. So far

Table: 7.3 : Physical Infrastructure in the village

Institution	*Available/ Not available*	*Condition at present*
ICDS/Anganwadi Centre	Available	Functioning Well
Primary School (Govt.)	Available	Dormancy/Not functioning
Electricity in the Village	Available	Functioning Well
Community Centre	Available	Infant Stage
Road	Available (Not Black top)	Functioning
Public Health Centre	Available	Dormancy/Not functioning
Veterinary	Available	Dormancy/Not functioning
Telephone	Available only Mobile (BSNL)	Functioning
Private School	Available	Functioning Well
Water Supply	Not Available	—
Livestock Aid Centre	Available	Dormancy/Not functioning
Transportation	Available	Functioning
Market Centre	Not Available	—
Post Office	Available in the Bazaar	Functioning Well
Bank	Available in the Bazaar	Functioning Well
College	Available in the next Village	Functioning Well
Internet	Available in the next Village	Functioning Well
Theatre Hall	Not Available	—
Club	Available	Infant Stage
Play Ground	Available	Functioning Well
Sale Centre	Not Available	—

Source : Survey

the road and transportation are concerned; National Highway 39 (Imphal-Dimapur) runs through Maram, it is approx 4-5 km from the Maram Khullen. Maram to Paren (in Nagaland) double lane highway expansion is under-construction in full swing; it is also just on the foothill of this village towards the south-west. The village is connected by a road (not tar/katcha) from Maram Centre (4-5 km from the village). Taxi (Sumo) or bus service is available from the village to Maram Centre or Senapati district headquarter once in the morning and return in the evening. But transport service very often disrupts in the rainy season. Otherwise villagers walk regularly from Maram Centre.

If we ask what is the most inconvenient/difficult problem in Maram Khullen the immediate answer will be drinking water.[7] And for health sector, one primary health centre is there in the village but it is not functioning because of the negligence of the villagers. The officer in-charge of this centre sits at Senapati district headquarter, never turn up in the village. If villagers need medical check up, they go to Maram Bazaar Public Health Centre or Senapati District Hospital. Interestingly, villagers spend less percentage of their budget on medical.[8] It may probably rely more on traditional healing system/herbal and hill villagers normally have strong immune system compared to city dwellers because of their regular movement/climbing.

If we are asked about physical infrastructure in Maram Khullen, there will be a dual answer. This means, everything is there but nothing is visible in reality. This village has got all basic physical infrastructures, which are very much necessary for a community to foster. But all these have drowned in the 'Tragedy of Commons'. In this regard, the role of community and the village leaders and politicians is very much significant.

Human Capital

According to Schultz (1965), 'Economic growth is largely the result of investment in human capital'. He argues that increases in the capital-income ratio are largely due to the human capital development, not material capital (i.e. reproducible, non-human capital), which was originally thought to account for all increases in income and subsequent economic growth. Human skill is the final determinant of economic development, which decides what type of method, technology or policy to be adopted in the development process. No matter how powerful the computer hardware or how user-friendly the software, most functions provided by computers (such as word processing, spread sheets, database management, computer-aided design, robotic manufacturing, and global positioning systems) still require hands-on human contact to be productive (Gordon 2000).

Porter (2000) opines that global competition and technological advancement necessitate that machinery and labour continuously change to meet consumer demand and competitive pressures. To accomplish this, global firms implement flexible organizational structures and high-performance work practices. High-performance work practices rely on skilled workers. In the opinion of Dreze and Sen (1996), human capital concerns the intrinsic importance of the quality of human life not seeing it just as an instrument for promoting economic growth and success. It incorporates education, health and skill.

Today, global competition and technological advancement necessitate that machinery and labour continuously change to meet consumer demand and competitive pressures. To accomplish this, global firms implement flexible organizational structures and high-performance work practices (in Weinberg).[9] So, skill and creative thinking labour has become a prime factor for efficient production. The same idea was also incorporated by classical economists right from Smith. The study of Dreze and Sen (1996) also suggests that the success in economic growth must ultimately be judged by what it does to human lives the quality of life human being can enjoy and the liberties they can exercise.

Whenever we talk about human capital, first it appears the idea of education, health and labour force in the picture. Maram Khullen in this section, almost all the components related to human capital has been discussed in the preceding chapters. For the present section, we are trying to analyze the strength and impediments of human capital and its role in the formation of village economy. It includes the level of employment and employability in the village.

Table 7.4 : Population, Education and Employment in the Village

No. of household	*Population (Excluding below 5 Years)*	*Educated persons*			*% of Population attained Higher*	*No. of Employees (Both private & Education**	*% of educated persons employed* govt.)*
		Matric	*Graduate*	*PG*			
432	2174	265	89	18	40.38	57	15.32

Source : Survey.

* Calculated from the No. of matriculate in the village.

The light of education has come in the village after 1980s with the establishment of Missionary institutions in and around the village. At the time of field survey (September 2006), there were 265 matriculates, 89 graduates (which consists of 75 in Arts, 8 in Science, 5 in Commerce and 1 in Medical), and 18 Post-Graduates (consisting of 12 in Arts and 6 in Science) in the village. With the available data, we could find out the percentage of persons who attained higher education from the number of matriculates, it was 40.37 per cent. The percentage of educated persons employed was 15.32 at the same period (Table 7.4).

Out of 89 graduates in the village, 12 of them are in the Arts, 6 in the Science, 5 of them are in the Commerce and 1 in the Medical. Employability limit in the village is not

Table 7.5 : No. of Persons in Higher Education and Employment

Stream	*Level of Education and No.*		*No. of Employment**
1. Arts	Graduate	75	7
	Post-Graduate	12	6
2. Science	Graduate	8	Nil
	Post-Graduate	6	4
3. Commerce	Graduate	5	1
	Post-Graduate	Nil	Nil
4. Medical	Graduate	1	1
	Post-Graduate	Nil	Nil
5. Technical	Graduate	Nil	Nil
	Post-Graduate	Nil	Nil
6. Management	Graduate	Nil	Nil
	Post-Graduate	Nil	Nil
Total	Sl. No. 1-6	**107**	**19**

Source : Field Survey

* Including employment in the Private Sector.

significant, so many of them got engaged in the cultivation. This level of education is quite high in a tribal village especially the level of higher education. It is perhaps due to the English education imparted by the private Christian Missionary Institutions. But the employability level is not that much high compared to the level of literacy rate in the village (51 per cent).

Persons who are self-employed are negligible and majority of them have taken up self-employment as driver by profession, driving taxi services locally. Majority of the villagers prefer government services and there is hardly any successful entrepreneur in the village. It is also clearly shown in the Table 7.5 that most of the educated persons are in the Arts stream. Research finding by Tilak (2005) and others have said that the private institutions cannot bring any quality education in the society. This may be the reason why the other technical degree holders are very much negligible. Still, it is much better than some communities in other States (as found in the author's earlier works).

Rainey and others (2003) observe, most rural communities have not effectively provided an advanced curriculum in primary and secondary education resulting into many have done a poor job of providing a basic education. The lack of access to basic educational opportunity has led to a workforce that has not been able to adjust to technology changes. Quality education determines the level of human capital. It is the most important component in the economic development in any nation. If this village likes to proceed to this direction, education should not be compromised at any cost. Unlike other urban areas, this village has less scope for business activities and almost all prefer secured salaried job. So, quality education should be given prime objective of the village in this competitive world.

NOTES & REFERENCES

1. Sagong is the traditional chief of the village (King). Mr. Kangnamba is the present Sagong of Maram Khullen and his mother Mrs. Hinga is the Queen of the village. She looks after the continuation of the traditional customs. Though she is like 'regent' she cannot involve village activities actively since she is a woman and old. Sagong (her son) takes charge of her responsibilities.
2. Khullakpa is the elected chief of the village but in case of Maram Khullen, Sagong itself is the Kullakpa. He is the hereditary Monarch in the village. By the Act of 1956, the Khullakpa became the ex-officio Chairman of the village authority.
3. There are three Sageis in Maram Khullen, they are : Mathak Sagei, Makha Sagei and Khullakpa Sagei.
4. The reasons for the failure of water supply and IFAD project have been discussed in the preceding chapters also.
5. At the time of field survey September 2006.

6. Inviting rain through ritual ceremony at the time of water scarcity period, traditional form of prayer before and after hunting at the time of annual village feast are some of the traditional practices still following even after conversion to Christianity.
7. Regarding water problem I have discussed in detail in the previous chapters.
8. For greater details, please refer to previous chapter.
9. As quoted by Rainey, D. V. *et al.* (2003).

8

Conclusion and Policy Implications

To conclude the information gathered by this research work, an attempt has been made to present the inferences and suggestions emanated from the study. To avoid repetition and duplicity of the chapters, information and analysis, a chapter-wise presentation of conclusion is made in the following paragraphs.

Moreover, on the basis of the understanding gathered through present research work, a modest effort is made to extend some recommendations which could lead to an improvement in the development programmes of this primitive tribal village. The recommendations are extended from the present research work as well as strategic management of the village economic structure.

Chapter 1 is an introductory one which deals with the research problem, objectives, methodology and chapter scheme of the present study. In this chapter, how to form a new tribal village, concept of village and the area of the present study are also included. The difference between tribe and tribal, scheduled tribe and primitive tribe are discussed clearly in the introduction.

This village is the home of the lone primitive tribe in the State. Their economy is closely linked with the agriculture and its allied activities. Though they belong to the primitive tribe and settler of hill village, their occupational structure has been undergone changed a lot in the recent past. They have completely given up shifting (*Jhum*) cultivation and not much related with forest activities. The level of education and literacy rate has gone up dramatically after the entry of Christian Missionaries.

This village is the biggest village among the Maram tribe and also one of the biggest tribal villages in the State. Total population of this village was 2374 at the time of field survey and 432 households were there in the village. The average family size is approximately 6 persons and the sex ratio is 925 female per thousand male. This village is a unique piece for understanding and analysis of tribal village.

Chapter 2 concentrates mainly on agriculture which constitutes village economy. Study of village economy without agriculture is like fish without water. Approximately 65 per cent of the family engage in agriculture. In this chapter, study on land ownership system, method of cultivation, cropping pattern and types of crop cultivated in the village are discussed. More interestingly, the role of women in agriculture is also incorporated at the end of this chapter.

The mode of cultivation and the cropping pattern has undergone a sea change with the emergence of globalization and modernization. Food processing and cultivation of commercial crop has already initiated in the village. Potato, ginger and passion fruit (horticulture) etc. are the main commercial crops. The traditional *jhum* cultivation has been discarded long before from this village. They have already started using modern technologies like power tiller for ploughing and truck (Shaktiman) for transportation of paddy.

Regarding the land ownership system, they have both individual as well as common or community land/property. Almost all the cultivable lands are owned individually and the rest which are basically forest and barren lands on the hill slope are owned by the community. Primitiveness in the economic system is still seen from the few examples like; they do not have standard of measure of land. The demarcation of land is made by river, mountain and forest etc. Despite being a tribal village, the volume of community land has been sinking day by day. Dispute over the common property between the villagers and clans is very common which leads very often to an individual land. The size of land by this village owned is quite sufficient if they want to live in a subsistence level. As the society develops the need or demand of the people has been growing and the pattern of consumption has changed greatly. This is the common phenomenon in almost all the village economies now.

Marketing problem of the village agricultural produces is seen in this village as well as in almost all the hill tribal villages. Mono-cropping pattern and the lack of agricultural infrastructures, e.g., transportation, cold storage, etc. are the basic stumbling block in the development of this sector in the village. In this context, contract farming and public-private partnership supported by the government in the field of basic physical infrastructure are the some solutions in this village. Work culture and peoples' participation is very essential for the village development especially for the tribal villages.

Chapter 3 deals with forest and water resources. The role of forest in the tribal village is very significant. Basically, forest provides fire wood for domestic consumption. Fire wood is also a major component of tribal life. Ninety per cent of the household uses fire wood for cooking purposes in this village. Regarding timber, they can use it for their self-consumption but not for commercial purposes. It is restricted by the State.

On the gloomy side of the study, water is one of the most important difficulties in the village. The survey result says that the average availability of water is 14 litres per head in the village. It is much lower than the average amount of water (20 litres) needed per head to lead a hygienic life. It is also found that the tragedy of water in the village is due to the negligence of the government and the lack of cooperation from the people of the village. Negligence of the government to provide basic needs of the villagers and the tragedy commons of public goods from the people's side are widely seen from the present study. These problems can be tackled by the proper management and support from the villagers.

Chapter 4 concerns with Health, Education and Population. These sectors are the indicators of economic development in any society. The exact size of population in this village cannot be ascertained because approximately 25 per cent of the households in the village have second house on the highway side or in the market area for the convenience of road and communication. Still, the size of population of this village is 2374 persons at the time of survey.

Coming to the Education sector, it has become the most important capital in economic development in the world. Educationally and spiritually, Christian Missionaries reincarnate the life of this village. The increase rate in higher education in general education in the village is approximately 40 per cent of the total educated people and the percentage of higher educated person employed is about 18 per cent in the village. This shows that the level of higher education is quite high compared to some of the villages in North East Region. It is the gift of Christianity in this village and the tribal community in general.

On the flop side of the study in this sector, this village could not precede much on the science and technical education. It is more or less same in other tribal villages also and the unit cost of education has gone up drastically due to the private education. In the field of Health, this village has been facing acute shortage of health facilities. They have got sub-public health centre as well as veterinary centre in the village. But these have not been functioning for long time.

These problems, like health and educational infrastructures can be solved by the people of the village or by the village council. Community and peoples' participation are very significant in this regard. Sense of responsibility of public goods and civic sense is to be inculcated. In this regard, inter-village or inter-community transfer of employees is very important. Nepotism, favouritism of the village council members is to be avoided, and more importantly, the political leaders should not interfere in this regard.

Chapter 5 deals with market and globalization. In this chapter, how globalization enters in the tribal hinterland and what are the consequences of it are widely discussed. Globalization enters in this village through market in the beginning. Globalization through market (globalization by road) could not do clean sweep in the tribal hinterland but the new wave of globalization (globalization by the air) did not sphere even the remotest village of the tribal. Despite having criticisms from the different scholars, the new wave of globalization has changed positively in the village. Moreover, no village or community can escape from the grip of globalization. So, it is beneficial for us to harness this process in a proper manner, otherwise we will be left behind by globalization.

Chapter 6 discusses the consumption pattern and source of income of the village. The highest contribution to the total income of the village (calculated from the 202 sampled households) is made by the agricultural sector amounting to Rs. 219 lakhs annually. It occupies a share of approximately 59 per cent to the total income in the village. Salary sector occupies second position in contributing village economy amounting to Rs. 61 lakhs, whose share to the total village income is approximately 16.48 per cent. The contribution of business or self-enterprise in the village economy is not that much significant, amounting to approximately Rs. 4 lakhs and occupies 1.08 per cent to the total income of the village annually. Despite having closely connected with forest and hill, the contribution of horticulture and forest to the village income is very meagre. They constitute 0.12 per cent and

0.22 per cent respectively (total to Rs. 0.48 and Rs. 0.81 lakhs respectively) to the village income.

On the expenditure side, the expenditure on food occupies highest percentage in the village income expenditure data sheet (Table 6.4). The approximate expenditure on food items is Rs. 190 lakhs, which constitutes 37.11 per cent of the total expenditure in the village. It is followed by consumer durable items which constitute around 23 per cent or roughly Rs. 117 lakhs. The next significant items are Non-durable consumer goods (Stationery items) and expenditure on education. They constitute 18.16 and 16.06 per cent respectively of the total expenditure in the village economy. These are roughly Rs. 93 lakhs and Rs. 82 lakhs respectively.

Except government employees category, rest goes to negative income balance in the village. It is perhaps due to the less importance in the investment sector. People give more importance in the unproductive expenditure. Banking habit is very negligible. The business sector side looks still gloomy in the village. Exploitation of local resources is very important. Work culture is to be developed among the villagers and business environment is to be inculcated in the village.

Chapter 7 concentrates mainly into three sectors like physical capital, social capital and human capital which are very much necessary for economic development in this globalization era. Very recently the concept of social capital has emerged as an engine to economic development. Development of a society cannot be determined only by physical resources. How the natural and physical resources are harnessed by the human and social capital is also discussed in this chapter. When we talk about human capital, education comes first in the picture. The level of education in this village is quite impressive due to the Christian Missionaries. The same point was also discussed in detail in the previous chapters. As far as Physical capital is concerned; this village has got almost all the basic pubic institutions, like school, health centre, veterinary centre, water supply, electricity, etc. Unfortunately, except electricity, the rest is not working in this village properly.

Basically, the tribal people are bounded by their social and community laws. It is same in this village also. The community law is more stringent than the State law. But this resource or social capital is not properly used in the economic activities. It has been proved by the failing projects in the village like, water supply, IFAD funded projects and public institutions etc.

Policy Implications

From the above few points, it is cleared that the necessary physical resources for economic development in this village are available. Now the problem that lies in this village is to harness the resources into a proper manner. The village has transformed a lot in the recent past in the field of education, occupation and transport and communication. When we look at the some other non-tribal villages in the region, this village is not that much primitive as we perceived. Since they are in the transitional stage of development, a dual characteristic of economy is found in the village. The strong social capital and the quality education definitely will take care of the arrested economic activities of this village. The positive aspect of this village is that the level of education is heading towards right direction. Definitely, this village will lead to a new height sooner or later. The programme like Communitisation of public sectors[1] is quite advisable in this type of tribal village. More importantly, the role of government and its functionaries are very much significant for the development of village economy. Some of the definite policy initiatives needed on the priority basis are :

1. Quality education which includes science and technical education is to be given more emphasis.
2. Communitisation of public institutions is to be initiated at the earliest possible.
3. Community leaders including the Village Chief is to be given proper and constant training for village development.
4. Government intervention in the development activities, especially in initialising public institutions is needed.
5. Social audit of the funded projects in the village is necessary for smooth and proper functioning of the schemes.
6. Government intervention in the traditional laws is also needed.

In this context, the study of village economy has become need of the hour for the region's further policy implication and future research in the field. Without in-depth micro study, formation of village development framework is an illusive agenda. Keeping this in mind, the present research work has been initiated in a typical tribal village (Maram Khullen), of a Primitive Tribe (Maram) of Manipur. Hope, this study will help in further policy implications and other similar research works in future.

NOTE & REFERENCE

1. Communitization is the programme which gives responsibility of the public institutions to the community. This programme has been initiated successfully in Nagaland.

Bibliography

Books

Ao, A. L. (1993): *Rural Development in Nagaland*, Har-Anand Publications, New Delhi.

Arrow, K. J. (1974): *The Limits of Organization*, Norton, New York.

Athickal, Joseph (1992): *Maram Nagas : A Socio-cultural Study*, Mittal Publications, New Delhi.

Bag, G. N. (2001): *Rural Transformation in Tribal Area*, Akansha Publishing House, New Delhi.

Barpujari, H. K. (2004): *The Comprehensive History of Assam* Vol. I (ed.), Publication Board, Assam, Guwahati.

Beardsley, Richard K. *et al*. (1959): *Village Japan*, University of Chicago Press, Chicago.

Bhagwati, Jagdish (2006): *In Defense of Globalization*, Oxford University Press, New Delhi.

Bliss, C.J. and Stern, N.H. (1982): *Palanpur — the Economy of an Indian Village*, Oxford University Press, New Delhi.

Boeke, J. H. (1953): *Economics and Economic Policy of Dual Societies: As Exemplified by Indonesia*, Institute of Pacific Relations, New York.

Chaudhari, Sarit K. and Chaudhari, Sucheta Sen (2005 eds.): *Primitive Tribes in Contemporary India* (in Two Volumes), Mittal Publications, New Delhi.

Dasgupta, Biplab (1978 ed.): *Village Studies in the Third World,* Hindustan Publishing Corporation (India), New Delhi.

Deb, Bimal J. (2002 ed.): *Development Priorities in North East India,* Concept Publishing Company Pvt. Ltd., New Delhi.

Deogaonkar, S. G. (1994): *Tribal Administration and Development with Ethnographic Profiles of Selected Tribes,* Concept Publishing Company Pvt. Ltd., New Delhi.

Doshi, S. L. and Jain, P. C. (1999): *Rural Sociology,* Rawat Publications, Jaipur.

Dreze, Jean and Sen, Amartya (1996): *India : Development and Social Opportunity,* Oxford University Press, New Delhi.

Dreze, Jean and Sen, Amartya (2006): *India : Development and Participation,* Oxford University Press, New Delhi.

Dumont, R. (1957): *Types of Rural Economy,* Methuen and Co., New York.

Fukuyama, Francis (1992): *The End of History and the Last Man,* New York Free Press, New York.

Gudeman, Stephen (1978): *The Demise of a Rural Economy : From Subsistence to Capitalism in a Latin American Village,* Routledge, London.

Hann, C.M. (1980): *Tazlar: A Village in Hungary,* Cambridge University Press, London

Haq, M. Nurul (1973): *Village Development in Bangladesh : A Study of Monagram,* Bangladesh Academy of Rural Development, Comilla.

Haswell, M.R. (1967): *Economics of Development in Village India,* Routledge and Kegan Paul, London.

Hayami, Yujiro and Godo, Yoshihisa (2006): *Development Economics : From the Poverty to the Wealth of Nations,* Oxford University Press, New Delhi.

Hayami, Yujiro and Kikuchi, M. (1981): *Asian Village Economy at Crossroads : An Economic Approach to Institutional Change,* Johns Hopkins University Press, Maryland.

Hayami, Yujiro *et al.* (1990): *Towards an Alternative Land Reform Paradigm : A Philippine Perspective,* Ateneo De Manila University Press, Philippine.

Hickey, Gerald Cannon (1964): *Village in Vietnam,* Yale University Press, New Havena.

Jain, P. C. (2001): *Globalization and Tribal Economy,* Rawat Publications, Jaipur.

Jeyaseelan, L. (1996): *Impact of the Missionary Movement in Manipur,* Scholar Publishing House, New Delhi.

Jogdand, P. G. and Michael, S. M. (2003 eds.): *Globalization and Social Movements — Struggle for Humane Society,* Rawat Publications, Jaipur.

Keith, Griffin (1974): *The Political Economy of Agrarian Change : An Essay on Green Revolution,* Harvard University Press, London.

Krishnamurthy, J. (2000): *Rural Development : Challenges and Opportunities,* Rawat Publications, Jaipur.

Madan, Vandana (2004 ed.): *The Village in India,* Oxford University Press, New Delhi.

Mehta, Basant and Jain, Navneet Kumar (2001): *A New Horizon for Rural Development : Service Area Approach,* Anmol Publications (P) Ltd, New Delhi.

Mohanty, P. K. (2002): *Development of Primitive Tribal Groups in India,* Kalpaz Publications, New Delhi.

Nanjundappa, D.M. and Sinha, R.K. (1982 eds.): *Backward Area Development : Problems and Prospects,* Sterling Publishers (P) Ltd., New Delhi.

National Institute of Community Development (1991): *Development and Change in Basudha : A West Bengal Village,* NICD, Hyderabad.

Nayar, B. R. (2006): *India's Globalization : Evaluating the Economic Consequences,* East-West Centre, Washington

Petra, Weyland (1993): *Inside the Third World Village*, Routledge, London

Putnam, R. D. (1993): *Making Democracy Work : Civic Traditions in Modern Italy, Princeton* University Press, Princeton NJ.

Radwan, Samir and Lee Eddy (1986): *Agrarian Change in Egypt : An Anatomy of Rural Poverty*, Croom Helm, London.

Ramaiah, P. (1981): *Tribal Economy of India : A Case Study of Koyas of Andhra Pradesh*, Light and Life Publishers, Delhi.

Ramamani, V.S. (1988): *Tribal Economy : Problems and Prospects*, Chugh Publications, Allahabad.

Rath, Govinda Chandra (2006 ed.): *Tribal Development in India : The Contemporary*, Sage Publication India (P) Ltd., New Delhi.

Richard K. Beardsley, John W. Hall and Robert E. Ward (1959): *Village Japan*. The University of Chicago Press, Chicago.

Sahu, Chaturbhuj (2002): *Tribes of North East India : An Ethnographic Profile*, Sarup and Sons, New Delhi.

Saran, A.B. (1997): *Contemporary Society : Tribal Studies*, Vol. 2. Concept Publishing Company Pvt. Ltd., New Delhi.

Sharma, B.D. (1978): *Tribal Development : the Concept and the Frame*, Prachi Prakashan, New Delhi.

Sikidar, Sujit (1990): *Economic Development of Tribal India*, Ashish Publishing House, New Delhi.

Singh, M. Romesh (2006): *Tribal Development in 21st Century*, Mittal Publications, New Delhi.

Singh, Awadesh Kumar (2003): *Dynamics of Tribal Economy*, Serials Publications, New Delhi.

Tomlinson, John (1999): *Globalization and Culture*, Chicago University Press, Chicago.

Tylor, J. Edward and Adelman, Irma (1996): *Village Economies*, Cambridge University Press, USA.

Upadhyay, V.S. and Pandey, Gaya (2003): *Tribal Development in India : A Critical Approach*, Crown Publications, Ranchi.

Upadhyaya, K.K. (1989): *Semi Primitive Economy of an Indian Village*, Mittal Publications, New Delhi

Yogi, Anand Kumar (1991): *Development of the North East Regions : Problems and Prospects*, Spectrum Publications, New Delhi.

Article of Edited Volume

Barpujari, H. K. (1994): "*Growth and Development of Higher Education in NEI (1826-1947)*" in Kumar, B. B. (ed.) 'Higher Education in NEI', Omsons Publications, New Delhi.

Dasgupta, P. (1988): "*Trust as a Commodity*" in Gambetta, D. (ed.), 'Trust : Making and Breaking Cooperation, Relation', Blackwell, Oxford

Debnath, Chandan (2009): "*Peoples' Participation : A Key Effective Development*" in Singha (ed.) 'Village Development in NEI', Concept Publishing Company Pvt. Ltd., New Delhi.

Dube, S.C. (1978): "*A Deccan Village*'" in Srinivas, M.N. (ed.), 'India's Villages'., Media Promoters and Publishers Pvt. Ltd, New Delhi .

Dube, S.C. (1998): "*Development Designs and Tribal People*'" in Dube, S. C. (ed.), 'Antiquity to Modernity in Tribal India Vol. I', Inter-India Publication, New Delhi.

Deogaonkar, S.G. (2005): "*Primitive Tribes*" in Chaudhari, S.K. and Chaudhari, S.S. (eds.), 'Primitive Tribes in Contemporary India' Vol. II, Mittal Publications, New Delhi.

Ferro, M. *et al.* (2006): "*Policies for Pro-poor Growth in India*" in Basu, Kaushik (ed.) 'India's Emerging Economy', Oxford University Press, New Delhi.

Gupta, Shilpy (2005): "*Human Rights and Primitive Tribes*" in Chaudhari, S.K. and Chaudhari, S.S. (eds.), 'Primitive Tribes in Contemporary India' Vol. II, Mittal Publications, New Delhi.

Mathew, G. P. and Singha, Komol (2006): "*Globalization and Its Impact on Tribal Society in NE : A Study of Maram Khullen Village in Manipur*" presented at the National Seminar at Assam University, Silchar from 26-28, org. by Deptt. of Sociology.

Misra, P.K. (2005): "*Myth and Reality of the Concept of Primitive Tribes*" in Chaudhari, S.K. and Chaudhari, S.S. (eds.), 'Primitive Tribes in Contemporary India' Vol. II, Mittal Publications, New Delhi.

Saran, A. B. (1997): "*Changing Strategy of Tribal Development*" in Saran, A. B. (ed.), 'Contemporary Society Tribal Studies Vol. II', Concept Publishing Company Pvt. Ltd., New Delhi.

Singh, Bhupinder (1998): "*Primitive Tribal Groups*" in Dube, S.C. (ed.), 'Antiquity to Modernity in Tribal India : Vol. I, Continuity and Change Among Indian Tribes' Inter-India Publications, New Delhi.

Yumnam, Amar (2002): "*Traditional Self-governing Institutions of the Hill Tribes of Manipur : An Economist's View*" in Goswami, Atul (ed.), Traditional Self-governing Institutions among the Hill Tribes of NE India, Akansha Publishing House, New Delhi.

Journal and Reports

D'Souza, Errol (2004): "Contractual Arrangements in Academia : Implications for Performance", *Economic and Political Weekly*, Vol. XXXIX (21):2165-68.

De, Anuradha *et al.* (2002): "Private Schools for Less Privileged : Some Insights from a Case Study", *Economic and Political Weekly*, XXXVII (52): 5230-36.

Gordon, R. J. (2000): "Does the New Economy Measure up to the Great Inventions of the Past?", *Journal of Economic Perspectives*, Vol. (14): 49-74.

Granovetter, M. (1985): "Economic Action and Social

Structure : The Problem of Embeddedness", *American Journal of Sociology*, Vol. (91): 481-510.

Hardin, G. (1968): "The Tragedy of the Commons", *Science* (164): 1243-48.

Harrison, B. (1992): "Industrial Districts : Old Wine in New Bottle?" *Regional Studies*, Vol. (26): 469-83.

Mc.Culloch, Major W. (1859): "Account of the Valley of Munnipore", *A Section from the Records of the Govt. of India*, No. XXVIII, Calcutta.

North, D. C. (1994): "Economic Performance Through Time", *American Economic Review*, June, Vol. (84) : 359-68

Pangare, V. and Pangare, G. (2007): "Implementing the Rights to Water", *Yojana*, September Issue, Vol. (51) : 9.

Paugat, Sunil (2006): "Contract Farming" *Yojana*, September Issue, Vol. 50 : (47).

Porter, M. E. (2000): "Location, Competition and Economic Development : Local Clusters in a Global Economy", *Economic Development Quarterly*, February, Vol. 14 (1) : 15-34.

Rainey, D. V. *et al.* (2003): "Essential Forms of Capital for Sustainable Community Development", *American Journal of Agriculture and Economics*, August, Vol. 85 (3) : 708-15.

Robertson, Roland and Haque, K. H. (1998): "Discourses of Globalization", *International Sociology*, March, XIII (1) : 29.

Schmidt, Ella (2006): "Sustainable Community for Sustainable Development: A Case Study of the Mujeres Reunidas Co-operative in Hindalgo, Mexico", *Journal of Developing Societies*, Vol. 22 (4) : 379-400.

Schultz, T. W. (1965): "Investing in Poor People : An Economist's View", *American Economic Review*, May, Vol. 40 : 510-520

Seabright, P. (1993): "Making Local Commons : Theoretical Issues in Incentive Design", *Journal of Economic Perspectives*, Vol. (7) : 113-34.

Shaban, A. and Sharma, R.N. (2007): "Water Consumptions in Domestic Households in Major Cities", *Economic and Political Weekly*, June 9, Vol. XLII (23) : 3218-25.

Shah, K. R. (2006): "State Inaction in Education in India" *Journal of Educational Planning and Administration*, XX (4) : 461-72.

Singha, Komol (2006): "Educated Unemployment in Nagaland : An Assessment", *Southern Economist*, 45 (14) : 21-24.

Singha, Komol (2007): "Highest Population Growth Rate : Is It an Issue?", *Southern Economist*, Vol. 46 (6) : 14-16

Shimray, U. A. (2003): "Demo(cracy) graphy and Ethnicity", *The Imphal Free Press*, No. (17) : 2.

Standing Committee on Labour and Welfare (2002): "Twenty-Eighth Report on Development of Primitive Tribal Groups", *Ministry of Tribal Affairs (Government of India)*, New Delhi.

Swaminathan, M. S. (2006): "Agricultural Renewal and Prosperity", *Yojana*, Vol. 50 (7), August Issue.

Swaminathan, M. S. (2007): "Agricultural Renewal", *Yojana*, Vol. 51 (89), January Issue.

Tilak, J. B. G. (2005) : "Higher Education in Trishanku : Hanging between State and Market," *Economic and Political Weekly*, XXXX (37): 429-37.

Tripathy, K. K. and Jain, S. K. (2007): "Agriculture in the Post-Reform Era : Issues, Challenges and Policy Options", *Kurukshetra*, 55 (9) : 3.

Woolcock, M. (2001): "The Place of Social Capital in Understanding Social and Economic Outcomes", *Canadian Journal of Policy Research* 2 : 1, pp. 1-17.

Index